Leadership Process Model

A Process-driven approach to becoming a more effective Leader

David Tuffley

Griffith University

To my beloved Nation of Four
Concordia Domi – Foris Pax

Management is doing things right;
leadership is doing the right things.
--Peter F. Drucker

Published 2011 by Altiora Publications
ISBN-13: 978-1456330453, ISBN-10: 1456330454

About the Author
David Tuffley PhD is a lecturer in the School of ICT at Griffith University in Australia. The content of this book is the product of research performed while an employee of Griffith University.

Acknowledgements
Special thanks are due to my partner Angela for her unwavering support and encouragement. Also to John and Nicola for listening patiently as we drove the long drive between Redland Bay and Brisbane on school days.

I also gratefully acknowledge Griffith University for allowing me to find my vocation and do a PhD on this subject, all rolled into one. My interest in leadership began as a child in the 1960's on hearing the speeches of John F. Kennedy and Martin Luther King, and wondering at the power of rhetoric to inspire and motivate millions.

Contents

Contents

Contents

Tables

A.   Introduction

Given the complexity of the global economy, the challenge of managing complex projects across dispersed geographical locations has never been greater. There is a clear need to find improved ways of managing this often difficult process now and into the future.

This book meets that need, giving you a structured and comprehensive approach to leading teams/projects, particularly when these are complex projects done by virtual teams.

By applying this Process Model for Leadership of Complex Virtual Teams, you can be assured that you are covering all of the most important activities needed to operate at an optimum level; and which could be very useful to know.

The principles outlined here are applicable to public and private sector organisations alike. Government departments with geographically dispersed offices, Commercial, Financial, Telecommunications, Educational, Health Care in fact any organisation operating virtual teams will benefit from this course, particularly where these teams are complex in nature.

A.1. How this book is organised

Part A: Introduction.

Part B: Review of leadership literature from which the model was derived. It is included for readers interested in a broad survey of the literature (both practitioner and academic) on the subject of leadership.

Part C: The Leadership of complex virtual teams process model. This is the central part of this book in which the process model is presented.

Part D: References.

A.2. Contact the author

The author welcomes feedback from readers. If you have comments, particularly constructive comments about any aspect of this book, you can contact the author on tuffley@gmail.com.

A.3. Some definitions of Leadership

Social influence. The Oxford English Dictionary defines leadership as the *ability to influence others within a given* *context.* A leader motivates others to achieve a goal. This quotation from Eisenhower sums up the process:

Leadership is the art of getting someone else to do something you want done because he wants to do it. [1].

Of the hundreds of quotes about leadership, this well-known quote from Eisenhower seems to exhibit best, though perhaps does not explain, the enduring enigma that is leadership. A manager may use authority to achieve compliance, but a leader finds a way to make the person *want* to do it. But how do we understand the distinction?

No commonly accepted definition of leadership. While leadership has been observed and studied for countless generations, little consensus exists as to what true leadership is. Indeed, on-going controversy exists between psychologists, sociologists, historians, political scientists and management researchers on this point [2]. Despite all of this time and effort, a universally accepted definition of leadership is yet to be developed.

Warren Bennis [3] observes that even after thousands of empirical studies on leadership over the past 75 years, no clear and unequivocal understanding has emerged as to how we can distinguish leaders from non-leaders. Clearly, the academic and practitioner thinking on this topic falls short of telling the whole story, hence the resorting to a baseline expert whose work has endured for 2,500 years as a good place to start our exploration of the true meaning of Leadership.

Nature or nurture? The thinking on leadership is somewhat polarised into two opposing views. Conventional wisdom maintains that leadership is an innate ability that natural leaders are born with, and which cannot be learned. A different school of thought, typified by Peter Drucker [4] and Warren G. Bennis [5], maintains that leadership can indeed be learned; that in effect, leaders are made rather than born. This is an underlying assumption of this book, and a view supported by the philosopher Plato who maintained In *The Republic* that the art of ruling (leadership) can be based on scientific principles and can therefore be learned [6]. The leader (ruler) uses the dialectic method to rationally analyse situations to determine appropriate courses of action informed by wisdom and understanding.

Leadership studies have been performed across the centuries in a wide variety of cultural contexts. Considering this sustained interest, it is reasonable to conclude that leadership is a fundamental aspect of the human species. It might be more accurate to say that there is an almost universal tendency for people to cooperate in groups in order to achieve outcomes that would be difficult or impossible for individuals to achieve alone, and for their efforts to be coordinated by a leader. Highly effective team-work and leadership might arguably be cited as a defining characteristic of the human species.

Virtual leadership in today's world. In the world of technology development, the business of managing complex projects across a variety of disciplines and geographical locations has never been more difficult, given the rising complexity of a global economic environment and the multi-national corporate entities that now inhabit this new world. There would appear to be a clear need to find improved ways of managing this often difficult process now and into the future.

A.4. Is it possible to describe Leadership as a process?

This section is only for people who wish to be persuaded that it is possible to describe Leadership as a process. It can safely be skipped by others.

A basic assumption of this book is that the factors and behaviors supporting effective leadership can be described in a process model.

There would be those who disagree with this proposition. Here, in summary, is why it is possible. The argument deals specifically with the Software Engineering domain, though given the generic nature of the argument there is no good reason to suppose that the principles involved are not able to be generalised across a wide range of domains.

In the business domain, Repenning and Sterman [7] notice a broad movement among 'managers, consultants and scholars' to recognize the value of understanding an organization's activities in terms of processes rather than functions. This tends to confirm the effectiveness of defined processes to solve the various challenges facing organizations.

Given this recognition of the usefulness of process, there is no observable reason [7] to suggest that process modelling could not be applied to leadership. Certainly, Total Quality

Management (TQM) emphasises the importance of leadership (along with human resource issues and strategic planning) to achieving success with TQM.

Humphrey [8] demonstrated the importance of leadership in the software development domain, including the importance of having managers learn leadership skills in his book *Winning with Software* Humphrey notes that as Director of programming with IBM he supervised 4,000 software professionals across many locations. His first step in transforming this extended team from one which had never delivered anything on time to one that did not miss a single commitment was to send 1,000 managers on a one week training course to establish effective practices [8].

A commitment to defined process in the software development domain, as typified by Humphrey [8] is reflected more broadly by W. Edwards Deming who is famously quoted as saying *'If you can't describe what you are doing as a process, you don't know what you're doing.'* [9].

The Model-based Process Improvement (MBPI) research effort in Software Engineering has generated a wide variety of process models over the past several decades [10]. This represents an elaboration on the commitment to defining processes discussed by Humphrey [8]. One weakness of process modelling is that as an abstract representation of reality, and not reality itself, they run the perpetual risk of being less than completely accurate. Inherent flaws not withstanding, they are arguably still worth developing and using, as drily observed in this well-known quote attributed to George Box that *all models are wrong, some are useful* [11].

Therefore if we accept the assertion that leadership can be learned rather than only be had through inheritance, then it is logical to assert that it can be described as a process, as suggested by Deming [9]. If leadership is describable as a process, it should then be possible to formulate these leadership processes into a Process Reference Model (that in the Software Engineering world must conform to the requirements of ISO/IEC 24774:2007 [12] and ISO/IEC 15504-2:2003 [13].)

Factors facilitating software development. There are many factors influencing software development, one of which is the existence of effective teams; another is the existence of defined processes to support the activities of the development team. The confluence of these two factors leads to the possibility of a process reference model for leadership comprising generic and specific leadership skills.

The logic is as follows:

Teams need leaders. Software in the modern context is developed by teams rather than individuals, particularly true in relation to complex systems [14]. Yet effective teams do not normally occur by accident; it is the actions of an effective leader that results in an effective team [4]. While not all activities performed by the team are done by the leader, it is ultimately the leader's responsibility to see to it that all of these activities are performed. Hence the leader is pivotal to project success [5].

Projects need defined processes. Software development is also facilitated by defined process (Humphrey, 2002). Without clearly defined and understood processes, a development team cannot hope to bring about a successful project outcome (i.e. one that is on-time, within budget and with a minimum of defects) [8].

There is literature in the model-based process improvement discipline that details how to describe a process (Rout, 2003; Van Loon, 2004, ISO/IEC 15504-2:2003).

B.The leadership literature

Until 'kings were philosophers or philosophers were kings' there will be injustice in the world. (Plato)

The classical period of ancient Greece is widely recognized as having produced concepts and modalities that are the bedrock of western civilisation. The philosopher Plato (427-347 BC) in his renowned dialogue *The Republic* outlined certain leadership principles that Western administrative thinking has based itself upon [6] . Plato developed systematic administrative thinking for the efficient running of the city-sate (polis) which over time allowed the evolution of democracy. Plato described in detail the appropriate relationship between the State and individual citizens. This relationship was so close that it was not possible to think of a citizen living outside of his State[6]. The purpose (telos) of this State is to educate people to become 'good'. The State is like the human body in which parts complement each other and act harmoniously. In terms of organisational theory, Plato would be regarded as a pre-modern functionalist.

In perhaps his best known tract *The Republic* (Polis), Plato states that politicians are the rulers of the new ideal state because they have (or should have) real knowledge (episteme) of what is 'the form of good'.

The art of ruling (leadership) can be based on scientific principles. In other words, it can be learned. The leader (ruler) uses the dialectic method to rationally analyse situations to determine appropriate courses of action with wisdom and understanding.

B.1. Distinguishing leaders and managers

The terms leader and manager are sometimes used interchangeably, adding to the ambiguity surrounding the study of leadership. Yet studies of administrative science usually find the terms differentiated. How is this done?

Chaos and order. Abraham Zeleznik [16] in his seminal paper on leadership suggests that the differences between managers and leaders lie at a deep level of the human psyche. Attitudes towards chaos and order are the basis of the difference. A manager aims for stability and control, seeking to resolve problems quickly, sometimes at the cost of understanding the nature of the problem fully. Leaders, by contrast, accept or at least tolerate chaos and lack of structure so that they might perceive and come to understand the underlying causes of situations. In this sense, Zeleznik argues, leaders have more in common with creative thinkers such as artists and scientists than they do with managers.

According to Takala [6] what managers and leaders have in common is the ability to get things done. Takala distinguishes them by seeing managers as a kind of instructor who puts pieces together, and then manages the 'things'. A manager is primarily concerned with making an organisation function by evolving routines that serve the ongoing and sometimes changing purposes of the organisation. Takala [6] observes that management is an activity typical in *larger* corporations. But there is leadership in *every* organisation, and not only in business organisations. A leader is a person who takes care of people and emphasises in his/her activities the social psychology of the organisation. Takala [6] notes that this is a somewhat artificial but commonplace distinction made in the management literature between the two activities. He acknowledges however that a person who runs a business or leads an organisation acts situationally in both roles, sometimes a manager, sometimes a leader.

B.2. Social construct of leadership

The socially constructed view holds that leadership is a myth, a socially constructed agency that reinforces existing social beliefs about the need for hierarchy [17]. A consequence of this view is the de-skilling of people, the placing of them into positions of subservience in order that they might follow the leader. Evidence of this is seen in the popular wish for heroes and messianic figures who will save the people and usher in a brighter future [17]. Despite the rather bleak nature of this position, it can nonetheless be observed that members of some organisations do behave like 'alienated robots' in their work relationships.

B.3. Leadership qualities of great groups

Bennis and Beiderman [18] discuss at length the leadership qualities required in Great Groups. They observe that the nature of group leaders can vary widely. There are facilitators, doers, contrarians. Leaders are catalytic completers; taking on roles that nobody else plays and that are needed for the group to achieve its goal. They have an intuitive understanding of the 'chemistry' of the group and the dynamics of the work process. Furthermore they encourage dissent in the establishment and maintenance of a shared vision. They can distinguish between healthy, creative dissent and self-serving obstructionism.

Bennis and Beiderman [17] identify four behavioral traits of effective group leaders:

Provide direction and meaning. Group members are kept up-to-date on what is important and why their work makes a difference.

Generate and sustain trust. The group has trust in itself and its leadership. This allows members to accept dissent and tolerate the turbulence of the group process.

Display a bias toward action, risk taking, and curiosity. A sense of urgency and willingness to risk failure to achieve results.

Are purveyors of hope. Find tangible and symbolic ways to demonstrate that the group can overcome difficulties.

B.4. Competencies of effective leaders

Bennis [5] in a wide-ranging study determined that effective leaders display four distinct personality traits, and five specific competencies, the sum of which tends to manifest in strong and effective leadership:

Personality Traits	Competencies
Guiding vision	Technical competence
Passion	Interpersonal skills
Integrity	Conceptual skills
Daring	Judgment
	Character

No pairing order is implied by this table, it is a listing only.

Table 1: Traits of Effective Leaders.

Bennis [19] asserts that it is *character* that is the essential element determining a leader's effectiveness, saying *'leaders rarely fail because of technical incompetence'* but more so for lack of character [20].

13

Strong character can manifest in positive and negative ways, as the lessons of history inform us. Strong character makes for a strong leader, but character can be strong and negative/destructive. Offerman et al [21] relates that a person's character will be determined by the sum total of his or her values. Offerman et al [21] identified the source of an employee's dissatisfaction and disillusionment is often the particular values held by leaders and the actions that these values motivate.

Davis and Landa [22] surveyed workers across Canada, determining that 75% of Canadian employees did not trust their employers. Bennis [19] confirms the importance of trust by emphasising that employee confidence in leadership is critical in the workplace, saying that it is *the emotional glue that can bond people to an organization.*

Branham [23] surveyed 3,149 people who voluntarily quit their job to assess their reasons for leaving. The exiting employees cited the following common reasons:

- Disappointment,
- Frustration,
- Anger,
- Disillusionment,
- Resentment, and
- Betrayal

These negative emotions are thought to be responses to an unmet human need for:

- Trust,

- Hope,

- A sense of worth, and

- The need to feel competent

It might therefore follow that an effective leader is someone who is able to meet these fundamental human needs, avoiding the trap that awaits a less effective leader.

B.5. Effective management of technical people

The seminal figure of Watts Humphrey looms large in the history of software engineering. His contributions include the original Software Capability Maturity Model CMM-SW), Team Software Process (TSP) and Personal Software Process (PSP); all of which were developed while with the Software Engineering Institute's Process Program.

A lesser known, but nonetheless relevant work by Humphrey is *Managing Technical People [24]*. While this work is based on Humphrey's experience as a senior project manager with the IBM Corporation, rather than on empirical research, it serves as a validation device for empirical research, given his undoubted stature in the software engineering domain. 'Validation' is used here in the software engineering sense, meaning to check the truth and accuracy of something in the practical world.

To summarise the behaviors and qualities of effective managers of technical teams, Humphrey [24] observes that:

- **Vision**. The ability to clearly perceive a worthy goal in terms of organisational success, and which has the quality of making people want to be part of the effort to make it real.

- **Goals**. Identified from the vision and the ability to drive steadfastly towards their realisation.

- **Conviction**. The ability to overcome obstacles in the path towards goal achievement.

- **Attract followers**. The ability to persuade others to sign-up or otherwise commit to a project, subject to limitations of choice. Humphrey distinguishes between the power to control and the power to lead. The latter is a mutual relationship, while the former implies coercion.

- **Care about followers**. A leader manifests an interest in the lives of, and a concern for the well-being of those they lead (what has been called 'individualised consideration').

- **Transform followers**. To convince followers to dedicate themselves to a project, sometimes requiring great personal effort, the net effect of which is to transform all concerned into high-achievers who derive much satisfaction from the transformative process (elsewhere described as transformational leadership).

- **Transact followers**. Use transactional power (power to reward with increased salary, promotion, job assignments) to effectively motivate followers.

- **Lead from below**. The ability to motivate followers to act as leaders in their own jobs, regardless of how modest or limited in scope this may be. The cumulative effect is nonetheless powerful.

B.6. Underlying qualities of effective leaders

The qualities that inspire people to persevere in the face of great difficulty, that engender trust and a sense of worth among team members are not always readily identifiable. These are qualities that are not easily detected, but which are found in the best of leaders.

Champy [25] identify these underlying qualities as:

- Empathy,

- Personal responsibility, and

- Openness to discovering truth

B.7. Empathy

Macaluso [26] suggests that empathy is the secret weapon of corporate success, an indispensable quality for any successful leader. Empathy is described as the ability to see the world through another's eyes, to experience it as they would. 'To walk a mile in another's shoes'. Macaluso [26] says 'They use it to form strong relationships, pick up early warning signs, and recognize opportunities to influence.' It is this caring aspect of the leader that makes people want to stay with them, inspiring loyalty.

B.8. Personal responsibility

Effective leaders accept that the circumstances in which they find themselves are largely the result of their own previous actions. They recognise the cause and effect relationships that have created the current situation, and understand how to engineer future desirable effects by performing certain actions in the present. They do not blame others [26]. They are able to see how their behavior affects corporate vision and how their leadership can affect the profitability of the organisation. Effective leaders are proactive, rather than reactive, taking the initiative to improve matters [26].

B.9. Open to the truth

Effective leaders fearlessly search for truth, knowing that sometimes the truth will not be pleasant to face [26]. They encourage discussion and do not resile from the outcomes of those discussions. The value of truth is recognised as the supreme antidote to delusion, or wishful thinking.

Macaluso [26] concludes with the point that really effective leaders are those that maximise human capital by displaying empathy, personal responsibility and truthfulness in all of their dealings. These traits appear to engender in people a favourable emotional state that is the foundation for effective team operation.

B.10. Transformational vs. Transactional

Zhang, Fjermestad and Tremaine [27] identify two parallel dimensions of leadership: *transformational vs. transactional*, and *participative vs. directive*. These have been derived from a body of foundational work in the area of leadership styles in a virtual team context.

On the Transformational / Transactional dimension we see the Transformational element as comprising four behavioral components [28] [29] [30]:

- **Charisma or idealized influence.** The leader engenders in the members a sense of pride, respect, faith and respect, together with a sense of purpose/mission.

- **Individualized consideration.** The leader manifests a deep concern for the well-being of team members, and provides mentoring.

- **Intellectual stimulation.** The leader stimulates members to think in original ways, emphasising the triumph of reason over irrationality, and challenging established ways of thinking.

- **Inspirational motivation**. The leader creates high standards, communicating high expectations.

Continuing with the Transformational / Transactional dimension we see the Transactional element as comprising three behavioral elements[28] [29] [30]:

- **Contingent reward**. The leader rewards performance on the basis of it having fulfilled prescribed obligations.

- **Management-by exception**. The leader ensures the standards are met.

- **Management-by-exception (passive).** The leader adopts a *laissez-faire* attitude until non-compliance of standards has occurred.

B.11. Participative vs. directive

On the participative vs. directive dimension, Bass [31] defines participative leadership as the equalization of power and sharing of problem solving with followers by consulting them before making a decision.

Bass [31] defines directive leadership as providing and seeking compliance with directions for accomplishing a problem solving task. Participative leadership and directive leadership are considered parallel to transformational leadership and transactional leadership respectively.

B.12. Review of leadership findings

Zhang, Fjermestad and Tremaine [27] discuss at length the findings from various literatures about the distinctions that can be made between Transformational / Transactional and Participative / Directive Leadership styles. In particular, they relate the following:

Bass and Avolio [32] discuss that in general, supportive, encouraging communication from the leader to team members were made under participative leadership rather than directive leadership. In dealing with a semi-structured or poorly defined problem, proposed solutions were more forthcoming in a participative leadership situation. On the other hand, solutions to structured or well-defined problems were more forthcoming with directive leadership [32].

In terms of group effectiveness or potency, higher level transformational leadership resulted in greater effectiveness than lower levels of transformational leadership [33]. The group potency difference was larger when groups were engaged in interdependent tasks rather than independent tasks. Interdependence resulted in greater potency. Anonymous groups working under high transformational leadership and identified groups working under low transformational leadership were most effective [33].

Elaboration (or the extent to which work was developed to a higher degree of complexity) was observed to improve significantly; while originality improved marginally when higher levels of transformational leadership were present [34]. Moreover, identified groups or teams with high transformational leadership were more flexible than identified groups in low transformational situations. Flexibility tended to vanish when groups were anonymous [34].

Lim, Raman and Wei [36] indicate that anonymity by itself does not alter the effects of leadership style on (a) participation, (b) cooperation or (c) the originality of the solution. With transactional leadership, anonymity was negatively associated with participation and association due to social loafing (idle chit-chat, gossip etc), but it was positively related to originality of solutions when a group reward as opposed to an individual reward situation exists [36]. It appears that giving members time to engage in apparently idle communication when group-based solutions are rewarded results in more focussed outcomes. With transformational leadership, anonymity did not significantly change the rate or degree of participation, cooperation, and originality when a group rewards situation exists (as opposed to an individual rewards condition) [36]. Team member satisfaction with the leader did not apparently differ across leadership styles; however transactional leadership did appear to result in greater group efficacy and task satisfaction than does transformational leadership. These advantages associated with transactional leadership (over transformational leadership) diminished when anonymity was introduced.

Team members working under the influence of transformational leaders tended to produce quality over quantity [37]. Output improved, though the quantity of it decreased. Members also tended to be more satisfied and displayed greater group cohesiveness than those led by transactional leaders [37]. Leadership satisfaction (highest in the face-to-face setting) was relatively high in virtual environments that approached full-immersion. Transformational leadership was associated with higher levels of trust in the leader and value congruence [37].

McColl-Kennedy and Anderson [38] report that both participative and directive leaderships were positively related to degree of participation. These in turn produced higher team performance, but with paradoxically lower levels of leadership satisfaction. The positive relationship between participation and team performance as well as the negative relationship between participation and team performance became stronger as the problem turned to be less structured [38].

B.13. Leadership of virtual teams

The concept and practice of distributed work is not new, enjoying a long and colourful history as discussed by O'Leary, Orlikowski and Yates [39] in their extended case study of the Hudson Bay Company from 1670 to 1826. Yet it has been the advent and subsequent advances in communications technology that has been a critical enabler of the development of this organisational form and practice [40].

It has been observed [41] that distributed teams, (or virtual teams as they might be called), face particular problems in relation to leadership. Organisational and management research has focussed intensively on the issue of leadership, as seen in a previous section, yet there is relatively little research done thus far on the emerging challenge of leadership in virtual teams [41].

B.14. Leadership of knowledge workers

Discussion of leadership in the globalized economy of the 21st century is not complete without examination of the way in which the new generation of workers who contribute to the global economy are best led and managed. Arguably, project team members on complex virtual teams fall into the category of knowledge worker for the reasons discussed below.

Knowledge workers are broadly defined as persons contributing to the knowledge economy (a post-industrial, post-service economic system). They are self-motivated, challenge-seeking persons who capture, manipulate and apply knowledge to create value. Knowledge workers usually know more about their job than their manager or anyone else in the organisation, and who often do not consider themselves to be subordinates in the traditional sense [42]. Knowledge workers cannot therefore be managed/lead in the same way as industrial or service workers.

One of Australia's leading academics, Professor Glyn Davis is recognised as an outstanding leader in a knowledge environment, having been described in those terms by former Queensland Premier Peter Beattie [42]. Professor Davis, who is currently the Vice Chancellor of Melbourne University, says that leaders should not tell knowledge workers what to do, but rather need to understand *what* they do and then lead by persuasive vision. This can be effected by:

- The views and visions of the knowledge workers are aggregated and shaped into a consistent theme,

- A vision based on these embedded values is developed,

- The vision thus formulated is articulated *back* to the knowledge workers with empathy and enthusiasm,

- The leader demonstrates high credibility,

- An understanding of the business and,

- Clear support for the business,

- The leader must be perceived as the embodiment of the values of the organisation,

- The leader skilfully uses multiple channels of communication to convey a consistent message that makes people feel good about working for the organisation. (This sounds similar to Eisenhower's idea of leadership being about *getting people to want to do what it is you want them to do*).

Skryme [43] outline some guidelines for the leadership of knowledge workers, distilled from the management literature. At a high-level, the critical leadership factors are a well articulated vision, a clear understanding of the link between knowledge and business benefits, together with effective marketing promotion. The leader must have a deep belief in the value of knowledge management to the organisation, and a commitment to innovative thinking and acting (including the willingness to commit resources).

DuBrin et al [42] summarise the leadership factors for knowledge workers as follows:

- Individual development plans for staff,

- Acquisition of innovative projects,

- Team composition; multi-disciplinary roles and mentoring/coaching,

- Use of quality systems,

- Systematic project evaluations,

- Planning for both formal and informal communications,

- Culture in which success and failure are discussed openly,

- Specific knowledge may become redundant but the ability to learn always remains valuable to the organisation,

- Knowledge workers' values must be aligned with those of the organisation,

B.15. Leadership challenges for virtual teams

An in-depth study into the typology of virtual teams, and the implications therein for effective leadership is found in Bell and Kozlowski's (2002) work. This work proposes 11 distinct challenges for the leadership of virtual teams. It is interesting to note that there is significant overlap between these challenges (or propositions) and the integrated teaming practices of the CMMI-IPPD as will be seen.

As previously discussed in the section dealing with virtual team definition, it should be noted that for the purposes of this study 'integrated team' is a broad term that includes 'virtual team' as a subset.

Bell and Kozlowski [44] identify four broad categories of leadership challenge in virtual teams; *(a) temporal distribution, (b) boundary spanning, (c) life cycle* and *(d) member roles*. The categories are described in the following way [44]:

Category	Description
Temporal Distribution	Virtual teams operating in real-time use rich, synchronous communication media and temporal entrainment to effect performance management.
Boundary spanning	Individualised consideration for and performance management of team members who span different functional

	areas, organizations and/or cultures.
Member Roles	Members holding multiple roles within and across virtual teams.
Lifecycle	Performance management effectiveness is improved when team membership is stable and on-going, allowing time for relationships to be established and developed.

No specific order is implied in this table

Table 2: Four leadership challenges in virtual teams.

The table below elaborates the 11 propositions relating to leadership challenges in virtual teams outlined by Bell and Kozlowski [44]. They are grouped into the four categories discussed above.

Category	Leadership challenge
Temporal Distribution	Distributed virtual teams are more likely to use synchronous, richly textured communications media.
Temporal Distribution	Effective virtual team leaders are more likely to develop substitutes for face-to-face contact.

Category	Leadership challenge
Temporal Distribution	The more complex the virtual project, the more likely it will be performed in real time, not distributed time.
Boundary spanning	The more complex the task, the more likely the team will be distributed.
Boundary spanning	Virtual team boundaries will be less permeable in complex projects where established operating procedures and stable relationships are needed.
Boundary spanning	Effective team leaders are likely to create proactive performance management functions, AND be good at using technology to provide members with team development experiences.
Boundary spanning	Effective leaders are good at evaluating the effectiveness of self regulation mechanisms, AND that these developmental functions will be more difficult to implement across multiple boundaries.
Boundary	More complex projects are likely to

Category	Leadership challenge
spanning	require stable team membership.
Member Roles	More complex projects are likely to require clearly defined singular roles for members.
Member Roles	Multiple roles and boundaries are likely to make performance management more difficult, AND effective leaders are more likely to clearly specify roles and role interrelationships, particularly in more complex projects.
Lifecycle	Discrete life cycle of virtual projects will be experienced integrated difficulty with establishing performance regulating functions, AND leaders will therefore focus on the most critical issue of establishing effective working relationships with members.

Table 3: Eleven leadership challenges in virtual teams.

B.16. Challenges of global software development

Holmstrom et al [45] discuss three kinds of distance in the arena of global software development – temporal, geographical, and socio-cultural – and present a useful view of how this distance dimension can relate to the software development process dimension. While this is not specifically about leadership, it can be argued that like the integrated teaming material from the CMMI-IPPD, these factors represent leadership challenges. An effective virtual team leader will find ways to address these issues effectively.

It can be seen also that there is overlap with the explicit leadership challenges outlined by Bell and Kozlowski [44] (see previous sections).

The table below outlines Holmstrom et al's [45] view of the interaction between the distance and software development process dimensions.

	Distance Dimension		
	Temporal Distance	**Geographical Distance**	**Sociocultural Distance**
Comm-unication	+ Improved record of communication	+ Potential for closer proximity to and utilization of remote skilled workforce	+ Potential for innovation and sharing best practice

		- Reduced opportunity for synchronous communication	- Increased cost and logistics of holding face-to-face meetings	- Risk of misunderstandings
Impact on GSD Process	Coord-ination	+ Decreased coordination needs due to division of labour	+ Increase in size and skills of labour pool can offer more flexible coordination planning	+ Access to rich skill set and various practices
		- Increased coordination costs	- Reduced informal contact can lead to lack of task awareness	- Inconsistency in work practices can impinge on effective coordination , as can reduced cooperation through misunderstandings
	Control	+ opportunities for round-the-clock development	+ Communication channels often leave an audit trail	+ Access to rich skill set and authority
		- Management of project artefacts may be subject to delay	- Difficult to convey vision and strategy	- Different perceptions of authority/hierarchy can undermine morale

32

Note + (plus sign) indicates an opportunity, - (minus) indicates a challenge.

Table 4: Distance and development process dimensions.

B.17. Effective virtual team leadership

Zhang, Fjermestad and Tremaine [27] in their review of earlier virtual team leadership studies suggest that given the inconsistencies inherent in the results, that a 'contingency' approach to studying team leadership might be appropriate. Contingency in this context refers to there being no single set of leadership skills that bring about effective virtual team leadership; rather that effectiveness is contingent upon contextual variables and situational complexity.

The contextual variables identified by Zhang, Fjermestad and Tremaine (2005) from their review of the literature include:

- **Communication media richness facilitating Trust.** The technology's ability to provide an environment that provides a rich perceptual experience for the participants. This includes immediate feedback, the number of perceptual cues and communication channels used, and the personalization of messages. Media richness facilitates trust between leadership and team member by minimising team process degradation while maximising motivation and commitment to a successful project outcome.

- **Goal-frustrating events managed by Optimism.**
  Obstacles and set-backs like technical problems,
  deadline pressures that threaten the accomplishment
  of the prescribed project objectives. This creates
  negative affect among team members, which can
  amplify itself over time to create a significant problem
  for the team. Inspirational motivation, optimism,
  individualized consideration and contingent reward
  all appear to optimise team performance by creating a
  positive affective climate.

- **Leader/follower gender, improved individualised
  consideration.** Female leaders have been shown to
  improve virtual team performance by exhibiting a
  higher degree of Individualized consideration
  behavior which causes higher levels of team
  satisfaction with the leadership. Combining
  individualized consideration with contingent reward
  further improves the leadership effectiveness of
  female virtual team leaders. In addition, in female-
  only groups, the effect of a charismatic virtual team
  leader is enhanced through effective trust-building.

B.18. Sloan Distributed Leadership Model

Ancona, Malone, Orlikowski and Senge [46] at the Sloan
School of Management have developed a Distributed
Leadership Model that offers an approach to understanding
and practicing leadership.

The Sloan Model basically outlines four dimensions of leadership [46]:

Sense making -- the process of making sense of the world around us, understanding the context in which we are operating:

- Get data from multiple sources: customers, suppliers, employees, competitors, other departments, and investors.

- Involve others in your sense making. Say what you think you are seeing, and check with people who have different perspectives from yours.

- Use early observations to shape small experiments in order to test your conclusions. Look for new ways to articulate alternatives and better ways to understand options.

- Do not simply apply existing frameworks but instead be open to new possibilities. Try not to describe the world in stereotypical ways, such as good guys and bad guys, victims and oppressors, or marketers and engineers.

Relating -- developing strategic relationships within and across organizations:

- Spend time trying to understand others' perspectives, listening with an open mind and without judgment.

- Encourage others to voice their opinions. What do they care about? How do they interpret what's going on? Why?

- Before expressing your ideas, try to anticipate how others will react to them and how you might best explain them.

- When expressing your ideas, don't just give a bottom line; explain your reasoning process.

- Assess the strengths of your current connections: How well do you relate to others when receiving advice? When giving advice? When thinking through difficult problems? When asking for help?

Visioning-- creating a compelling and feasible vision of the future as it might apply to the organization

- Practice creating a vision in many arenas, including your work life, your home life, and in community groups. Ask yourself, 'What do I want to create?'

- Develop a vision about something that inspires you. Your enthusiasm will motivate you and others. Listen to what they find exciting and important.

- Expect that not all people will share your passion. Be prepared to explain why people should care about your vision and what can be achieved through it. If people don't get it, don't just turn up the volume. Try to construct a shared vision.

- Don't worry if you don't know how to accomplish the vision. If it is compelling and credible, other people will discover all sorts of ways to make it real –ways you never could have imagined on your own.

- Use images, metaphors, and stories to convey complex situations that will enable others to act.

Inventing – creating new ways of working together to realize the vision.

- Don't assume that the way things have always been done is the best way to do them.

- When a new task or change effort emerges, encourage creative ways of getting it done.

- Experiment with different ways of organizing work. Find alternative methods for grouping and linking people.

- When working to understand your current environment, ask yourself, 'What other options are possible?'

- All of the previous paragraphs derived from Ancona, Malone, Orlikowski and Senge, [46]

- The authors go on to describe the indications of when these activities are not being performed well:

Signs of weak sense making

- You feel strongly that you are usually right and others are often wrong.

- You feel your views describe reality correctly, but others' views do not.

- You find you are often blindsided by changes in your organization or industry.

- When things change, you typically feel resentful. (that's not the way it should be!)

Signs of weak relating

- You blame others for failed projects.

- You feel others are constantly letting you down or failing to live up to your expectations.

- You find that many of your interactions at work are unpleasant, frustrating, or argumentative.

- You find many of the people you work with untrustworthy.

Signs of weak visioning

- You feel your work involves managing an endless series of crises.

- You feel like you're bouncing from pillar to post with no sense of larger purpose.

- You often wonder, 'Why are we doing this?' or 'Does it really matter?'

- You can't remember the last time you talked to your family or a friend with excitement about your work.

Signs of weak inventing

- Your organization's vision seems abstract to you.

- You have difficulty relating your company's vision to what you are doing today.

- You notice dysfunctional gaps between your organization's aspirations and the way work is organized.

- You find that things tend to revert to business as usual.

- All of the previous paragraphs derived from Ancona, Malone, Orlikowski and Senge, [46].

B.19. Integrated team leadership & CMMI-IPPD

The Capability Maturity Model Integration (CMMI) developed by the Software Engineering Institute at Carnegie-Mellon University contains detailed material in relation to integrated teaming without mentioning leadership specifically. And yet, when the nature and scope of this material is examined, it becomes apparent that much of this Integrated Product and Process Development (IPPD) material describes *de facto* leadership practices. These are activities that must be performed by someone. If a leader takes ultimate responsibility for successful project outcomes, it is he or she that is responsible for making sure these activities are done.

The CMMI-IPPD is derived from the IPD-CMM (Integrated Product Development Capability Maturity Model) developed by Suzanne Garcia of the Software Engineering Institute in the 1990's. Looking further back, IPD-CMM itself derived from Concurrent Engineering from the 1980's, which can trace its origins back to the late 19th Century. This chronology is mentioned to indicate the strength and accumulated wisdom of CMMI-IPPD.

What follows is an adaptation of the goals and practices from CMMI-IPPD to have a leadership-orientation. The original CMMI-IPPD Specific Goal and Practice numbers are included for reference purposes.

An effective leader of an integrated team will:

Establish the project's work environment (IPM+IPPD SP1.3) by creating an environment in which all virtual team members have access to and use (preferably broadband) two-way communications media.

Establish the project's shared vision (IPM+IPPD SP3.1) by understanding and communicating to team members the mission, goals expectations and constraints of the project in a way that creates a sense of common purpose and enthusiasm.

Establish the integrated team structure (IPM+IPPD SP3.2) by considering the nature and scope of the project to arrive at an appropriate team structure (for example based on the product work breakdown structure). The team structure should be dynamic, able to adapt to emergent circumstances.

Allocate requirements to integrated teams (IPM+IPPD SP3.3) by assigning requirements, responsibilities, tasks, and interfaces to teams in the integrated team structure.

Establish integrated teams (IPM+IPPD SP3.4) within the larger team structure (team leaders and members assigned, team charter established, resources allocated).

Ensure collaboration among interfacing teams (IPM+IPPD SP3.5) by creating an environment of collaboration, informed by the shared vision, facilitated by communications technology and brought together by the leader with the help of interface control working groups.

Establish empowerment mechanisms (OPD+IPPD SP2.1) that allow team leaders and members to recognise clear channels of responsibility and authority. These mechanisms shall avoid situations where people assume too much or too little authority and when it is unclear who is responsible for making decisions.

Establish rules and guidelines for integrated teams (OPD+IPPD SP2.2) by maintaining a clearly defined set of criteria for structuring and forming integrated teams. These operating rules and guidelines define how teams interact.

Balance team and home organization responsibilities (OPD+IPPD SP2.3) by having clear guidelines for how members can balance their team and home organization responsibilities. A 'home organization' is the part of the organization to which team members are assigned when they are not on an integrated team.

C. Leadership process model

On our way to reaching this place where the essence of leadership can be expressed in simple cause and effect statements, we have travelled a long way in time. The greater the truth, the more simply it can be expressed, and the more enduring it will be.

The Leadership of Complex Virtual Teams Process Model is a general purpose model that is applicable to a broad range of projects. There are no specific exclusions to the kind of project to which it can be applied.

While the model is designed to apply to complex virtual teams, it can be similarly used for simple teams whose members are co-located (not virtual), complex co-located teams, or simple virtual teams. Any combination is workable.

The model is divided into three sections;

- Personality/character-traits of the leader,

- Team factors, and

- Organisational factors.

C.1. How to see this model

The model is an abstract representation of reality. Using this model is intuitive and designed to be easy to adapt to your own situation. But a model that can be applied to the broadest range of situations will by necessity be *abstract* in nature. It is an abstract representation of reality, not reality itself.

Tells you what, you decide how. This might bother some readers who prefer to be told exactly how to go about doing something. But this prescriptive approach rarely works as a 'one-size-fits-all' solution. A better way is for you to apply the model in your particular case after being told what the purpose of the process is, what outcomes you should have when the process is fully performed, and be guided by clearly laid out informative material that fills in the detail and puts it into context. This approach recognises that *you* are the best person to decide how to go about things, the process model just tells you *what* you should be doing in a best-practice sense.

Leadership is situationally expressed. Supporting the process model approach is the fact that despite thousands of research studies performed over decades, even centuries; no-one has yet come up with a definition of leadership that everyone can agree on. This is because leadership is expressed uniquely according to the circumstances in which it occurs. But beneath the world of appearances are the underlying essential factors that must be present for leadership to be expressed. That is what this model is, the essential underlying factors that you can use to guide your own efforts to manifest leadership in your own world in your own way.

The essence of leadership. Do not believe people who say leadership is something you are born with and which cannot be learned. It is true that certain individuals are born with charisma and for whom leadership seems to come easily. Whether you are one of these people or not, the principles of leadership, once understood, can be applied in one's own life to good effect. What is required is the commitment to improving one's practice, critically evaluating one's own way of doing things and being prepared to change. Not always an easy thing to do, given that we tend to invest heavily in our established habits and dislike change because it threatens that investment.

For reference purpose only, the following ISO standards were used in the development of this model:
ISO/IEC 12207:2004, Information technology — Software life cycle processes
ISO/IEC 15504-1:2004, Information technology — Process assessment — Part 1: Concepts and vocabulary
ISO/IEC 15504-2:2003, Information technology — Process assessment — Part 2: Performing an assessment ISO/IEC 24774:2007 Software & systems engineering -- Life cycle management -- Guidelines for process description

C.2. How to use this model

Be sure to read this section carefully.

C.2.1. How the model is structured

Each process contains the following elements in the order shown:

Identifier & Name – each process is uniquely described (eg. IND.1) and named (eg Vision)

Process Purpose -- the underlying *intention* of the process.

Process Outcomes -- a list of activities that if performed will achieve the purpose

Base Practices – the Outcomes expressed in behavioral terms (what you should actually do to the achieve the outcome)

Work Products / Activities / Conditions – a list of inputs and outputs that achieve the outcomes, or put another way, that which is consumed and produced in the performance of the base practices.

Informative Notes – describe in plain language what each outcome means to help you understand not just the content but the spirit of the outcome. The Informative Notes also includes a more *general discussion* to assist further with understanding the process, followed by a section on how this process applies in the case of *Virtual and/or Integrated Teams*.

45

C.2.2. Step 1: Commitment to implementing change

Study the overall content and organisation of the model and develop a strong sense of determination that you will implement it and so transform yourself into a more effective leader than you currently are.

The ordering of the processes is significant, and indicates a general sequence, though some flexibility is allowed. For example, an effective leader must first have a compelling vision of some desirable future state, and have the ability to communicate this vision to people in a way that makes them want to be part of the effort to realise the vision. Objectives derive from the vision and so on.

The Team leadership factors likewise express a sequence; as does the Organisational factors. You should get an understanding of the flow of activities for each group (IND, TEM, ORG).

Individual Process Group (IND)

IND.1 Vision
IND.2 Objective(s)
IND.3 Integrity
IND.4 Action-orientation
IND.5 Intelligence
IND.6 Individualized consideration
IND.7 Management-by-exception

Team Process Group (TEM)

TEM.1 Team structure

TEM.2 Team requirements

TEM.3 Team recruitment

TEM.4 Team environment

TEM.5 Team formation

TEM.6 Team roles

TEM.7 Team rules

TEM.8 Team authority

TEM.9 Team performance management

TEM.10 Team development

Organisation Process Group (ORG)

ORG.1 Team boundaries

ORG.2 Team collaboration

ORG.3 Team & home organization balance

C.2.3. Step 2: Read each process carefully

Set aside a 10 or 15 minute period to read, understand, and digest each process.

Read each process carefully from start to finish, all the way to the end of the informative section.

As you do this, the question *'how would this best apply in my own case/project?'* should be uppermost in your mind. Make implementation notes in the column provided.

For best results, do not rush. This is a self-reflective process which cannot be rushed if it is to succeed.

C.2.4.   Step 3: Apply processes progressively

After reading carefully through each process, taking the time to understand and make notes about how it might apply in your own case/project:

Beginning with *IND.1 Vision,* focus intensely on each Base Practice and formulate in your mind a clearly understood way that you can see to perform this practice. See yourself doing it in your mind's eye.

Be very specific; do not gloss over a practice with the intention of coming back to it. Focus on each Practice in sequence in a methodical and disciplined way.

Spend about a day working on each process. Doubtless there will be other matters to attend to during the course of the day, but as an on-going activity, use that day to perform step 1 (above) on a particular Process and its Base Practices.

Accept that it will be three weeks or more before you reach the last process. Studies in Cognitive Psychology indicate that transformations in people's habits/thinking take around two weeks or more to become firmly established.

Cultivate the patience and the discipline to work through the process model in the way indicated here. Understand that this steady, incremental approach is an excellent way to bring about lasting change.

Make detailed notes as you go in the Notes section.

C.2.5. Step 4: Fill in the gaps

As you work through the processes and their associated outcomes, you will notice that some of them you are already doing, and some of them you are not doing:

Use the model as a comprehensive guide. If you follow it, you have a reasonable assurance that you are not leaving anything important out.

Those processes and outcomes that you are already doing might have room for improvement by adding or amending to the existing activities listed in the *Work products / activities / conditions* section of each process.

The rest, those that you are not doing, should be where the focus of your effort lies. Work progressively to fill in these gaps. Remember, it is steady, incremental change that you should be aiming for, not radical change in a short period. The former is sustainable and on-going, the latter rarely lasts for long.

C.2.6. Step 5: Reflect on progress & keep moving forward

After applying the processes progressively over three weeks, the challenge is to keep the improvement momentum going in the face of distractions. There is the inevitable desire to think about and do other things, new things. After all, we have a built in mechanism that seeks to maintain the status quo in our lives. The longer you focus on something, the more likely it is you will be changed by it and at some level you may not *want* to change. Attempts the change the status quo are likely to be seen as a threat.

Cultivate a monitoring, self-reflective mind-set in which part of you is always noticing what the rest of you is doing and thinking. With this comes the awareness of the linkages between cause and effect from past to present. You understand that the circumstances in which you find yourself today are the result of your actions and decisions in the past, and not due to some external entity over which you have no control.

This self-awareness is the foundation of self-improvement. By becoming more self-aware you are engaging areas of the brain that are capable of higher rational thought but which goes largely unused for much of the time in people operating on the level of instinct.

It is no coincidence that the attributes of vision, persuasive communication, integrity, goal-orientation, action-orientation, creative thinking etc are all attributes of a *self-actualised* person (after Maslow). You are learning to be a leader of yourself, and this is a prerequisite of leading others.

C.2.7. Individual Process Group (IND)

C.2.7.1. IND.1 Vision

Process ID	IND.1	Notes
Process Name:	**Vision**	
Process Purpose:	The purpose of the vision process is to create and communicate a shared vision in ways that inspires people to realise that vision.	
Process Outcomes:	As a result of successful implementation of the vision process:	
	1. A vision of the goal(s) is created.	
	2. The vision of the goal(s) is communicated to the team	
	3. Commitment by team to the shared vision is gained	
Base Practices:	**IND.1.BP1: Create the vision.** The leader envisions a desirable	

future condition [1]

IND.1.BP2: Communicate the vision. The leader communicates the vision in a way that creates positive expectation in the team members [2].

IND.1.BP3: Commitment to vision by team. The leader obtains commitment from the team members for the realisation of the vision, making it a shared vision [3].

Work Products / Activities / Conditions

Inputs	Outputs	Notes
Business goals [Outcome 1]	Team Charter [Outcome 1]	
	Imperative Objectives [1]	
Customer requirements [1]	Project Plan [1]	
	Project launch	

	presentation [1]
	Planning session with senior management [1]
Briefings from Senior Management [Outcome 2]	Vision statement communicated [Outcome 2]
	Roadmap (implementing vision statement) [2]
	Yearly kick-off [2]
Performance data [2]	Quarterly review [2]
Customer feedback [2]	Team briefing [2]
	Regular team meetings [2]
Commitment by team to the shared vision is gained [3]	Vision statement is communicated by management [Outcome 3]
	Team buy-in exercises [3]
	Project vision

communicated at launch
and reinforced
subsequently [3]

Informative Notes

Outcome 1 -- the vision of the goal is seen by the leader as achievable. The goals will still be abstract at this point. The goal(s) become concrete when translated into objective(s).

Outcome 2 – the shared vision should be communicated in a way that creates positive expectation and motivation among the team.

Outcome 3 – the way in which the shared vision of the abstract goal(s) is communicated should generate strong commitment to the achievement of the goal(s)

General

The shared vision is a clear and unambiguous expression of an envisioned future. It is the basis for a common understanding among stakeholders of the aspirations and governing ideals of the team in the context of that desired outcome. Conditional on being effectively communicated by the leader to the team, the shared vision grounds the team's governing ideas and principles and allows for appropriate objectives to be derived.

Highly effective groups are often convinced they are engaged in important work, sometimes nothing short of being on a 'mission from God'. The work becomes an abiding obsession, a quest that goes well beyond mere employment. This intensely shared vision and sense of purpose endows cohesion and persistence.

Creating and communicating a compelling vision of the future is an aspect of charisma; inspirational motivation, optimism, individualized consideration and contingent reward all appear to optimise team performance by creative a positive affective climate.

In summary when promulgating a shared vision, the following factors should be considered:

- the project's objectives
- the conditions and outcomes the project will create
- interfaces the project needs to maintain
- the visions created by interfacing groups
- the constraints imposed by outside authorities (e.g., environmental regulations)
- project operation while working to achieve its objectives (both principles and behaviors)

Virtual and/or Integrated Teams

In virtual environments the means by which the leader communicates the vision is of critical importance. Ideally, the virtual team should be brought to a single location for a team launch and team building exercise. Next best is high definition video-conferencing in conjunction with other channels of communication such as group-ware and email.

In integrated team environments, the complexity of the overall project team is likely to present practical difficulties in the means by which the leader's vision can be effectively communicated. As with virtual teams, the most effective method until fully immersive virtual environments are available is to bring everyone together at a project launch.

Team bonding activities can and should be organised at the launch. If such an event is not practical, then effective use of the available communications technology must be made.

Notes on how to apply in your project(s)

Table 5: IND.1 Vision

C.2.7.2.   IND.2 Objectives

Process ID	IND.2	Notes
Process Name:	**Objectives**	
Process Purpose:	The purpose of the objectives process is to create and communicate objective(s) based on the vision and derived goals.	
Process Outcomes:	As a result of successful implementation of the objectives process: 1. Practical objective(s) for goal(s) achievement are developed. 2. Positive expectation for achieving objective(s) is encouraged.	
Base Practices:	**IND.2.BP1: Develop objectives**. The leader derives a set of practically worded objectives from the shared vision and subsequent goals that give the team a concrete set of	

outcomes to achieve. [1]

**IND.2.BP2: Encourage
positive expectation**. The
leader generates an
optimistic mind-set and
outlook in the team
towards the achievement
of the objectives [2]

Work Products / Activities / Conditions

Inputs	Outputs	Notes
Vision statement [1]	Goals [Outcome 1]	
	Objectives [1]	
Project plan [1]	Goals [1]	
	Objectives [1]	
Project launch [2]	Positive expectation re vision [Outcome 2]	
Team briefing [2]	Commitment to vision [2]	
Yearly kick-off	Positive expectation re	

[2]	vision [2]
Quarterly review [2]	Commitment to vision [2]

Informative Notes

Outcome 1 – from the shared vision and subsequent goals described in the previous Process a set of practically-worded objectives are developed that give the team a concrete set of outcomes to achieve.

Outcome 2 – having developed concretely-worded objectives, the leader generates in the team an optimistic mind-set and outlook to wards the achievement of the objectives.

General:

Once the leader has developed a compelling vision of what is to be accomplished, and managed to communicate it in a way that generates enthusiasm and commitment by the team, the leader, in consultation with team members if practical, develops a set of practically-worded objective(s) of what is to be achieved.

Virtual and/or Integrated Teams

In virtual and integrated team environments the consultation process may be more difficult but is nonetheless important. The leader needs to get team member buy-in, or commitment, to the objectives, and this requires canvassing widely the views and attitudes of the team. The objectives must then be framed in a way that is consistent with those attitudes. The objectives are then fed back to the team. The team should recognise something of their input in what they receive.

Unquestioning obedience to orders coming down the chain of command is a necessity in the military, but is unlikely to work in a non-military environment, particularly where knowledge workers are concerned. Knowledge workers usually value themselves highly, often knowing more than the leader about their particular job. They require careful handling with an attitude of respect.

In virtual environments where the leader's presence is diminished, a good strategy is to lead by subtle influence -- allowing team members to exercise their sense of self-government, gaining influence by allowing them to feel influential.

Appearing to lack a compelling vision of the future will quickly undermine the confidence of the team for your leadership.

Notes on how to apply in your project(s)

Table 6: IND.2 Objectives

C.2.7.3. IND.3 Integrity

Process ID	IND.3	Notes
Process Name:	**Integrity**	
Process Purpose:	The purpose of the integrity process is to consistently act with integrity and competence over time in pursuit of the vision.	
Process Outcomes:	As a result of successful implementation of the integrity process: 1. Integrity is consistently practiced. 2. Competence is consistently exhibited.	
Base Practices:	**IND.3.BP1: Practice integrity.** The leader consistently displays integrity, characterised by openness to truth, trustworthiness, and adherence to principle [1]	

IND.3.BP2: Behave competently. The leader consistently manifests competence, characterised by technical and interpersonal skills, and advanced conceptual and reasoning skills. [2]

Work Products / Activities / Conditions

Inputs	Outputs	Notes
Perceived trust in leader [Outcome 1]	Team has faith in leader as expressed and demonstrated [1]	
	Team defends leader against criticism [1]	
Consistently honest behavior [1]	Leader is trusted inside and outside of the team [1]	
Principled in situations where 'easy way' is tempting [1]	Team can often predict leader's action / reaction in given situation [1]	

Understanding of technical issues [2]	Competent technical leadership [2]
Skilled at interpersonal communication [Outcome 2]	Team is kept unified and functional through leaders competent communication efforts [2]
Ability to abstractly conceptualise solutions (particularly technical, but also political) to problems/challenges [2]	Appropriate solutions to technical and political challenges are imagined then implemented by leader [2]
Ability to think logically [2]	Rationale solutions are devised based on a rational chain of reasons [2]

Informative Notes

Outcome 1 – the leader consistently displays integrity, characterised by openness to truth, trustworthiness, and adherence to principle.

Outcome 2 – the leader manifests competence, characterised by technical and interpersonal skills, and advanced conceptual and reasoning skills. Competence in this context can be seen as an aspect of integrity in that it would be dishonest of an incompetent leader to act in a capacity that requires competence.

General

Principle-centred leadership creates a climate in which team members can rely on a leader to act according to guiding principle rather than exigent circumstances. Involves doing the 'right thing' all of the time, even when it is easier not to under the circumstances.

Such a leader leads by example, leads by having an open, enlightened mind, leads by remaining true to him/herself. Such a person is a natural leader, one who is respected and whose example is followed. The antithesis is the tyrant who is closed-minded and who uses force to make people cooperate.

Such a leader acts from a sense of oneness with those being led. This sense of oneness is cultivated in a general sense by learning to recognise the interdependence and connectedness of the group members.

Such a leader avoids using unnecessary force to achieve ends, understanding that to do so create a new set of problems.

Self-worth is encouraged when the leader minimises the perceived distance between their sense of their own position and the position of those they lead. By identifying with the group members the leader can better understand the psychological needs of the members, and so their decisions are more aligned with those needs. By extension, an effective leader might go so far as to practice humility as a way of engendering the trust and respect of the group members. The interests of the members are naturally promoted because they are the interests of the leader as well. Therefore, effective leaders win the confidence of group members because the members sense the leader's identification with them.

Virtual and/or Integrated Teams

In virtual environments a leader's perceived integrity serves as a guiding and unifying influence to team members. Integrity engenders trust. Consistent integrity becomes something akin to a trusted presence in the mind of the team member, giving them a degree of certainty and helping to overcome the self-doubt that is sometimes inherent in an isolated work context.

In complex teams where members do not regularly encounter the leader, a similar benefit is observed. Integrity is defined in general as being whole and complete, with nothing missing. A leader who displays integrity is the embodiment of principled behavior; someone who can be relied upon to act in a principled way regardless of circumstance.

Integrity therefore calls for a high degree of moral courage, since from social psychology we know that people generally act according to who they are with rather than on principle, particularly if doing so will make them unpopular.

Notes on how to apply in your project(s)

Table 7: IND.3 Integrity

C.2.7.4. *IND.4 Action-orientation*

Process ID	IND.4	Notes
Process Name:	**Action-orientation**	
Process Purpose:	The purpose of the action-orientation process is to be inclined towards action and resilience.	
Process Outcomes:	As a result of successful implementation of the action-orientation process:	
	1. Objective-achieving behavior is decisively pursued.	
	2. Objective-frustrating events are met with resilience.	
	3. Viability of continuing pursuit of current objective(s) is evaluated.	
Base Practices:	**IND.4.BP1: Pursue objective-achieving behavior.** The leader consistently displays the	

ability to think and act decisively in pursuit of objective(s) [Outcome 1].

IND.4.BP2: Resilient when objectives are frustrated. When progress is frustrated the leader consistently displays a willingness to try again until success is achieved [Outcome 2].

IND.4.BP3: Evaluate on-going viability of objectives. The leader rationally evaluates whether continued pursuit of current objectives is advisable or needs revision [3].

Work Products / Activities / Conditions

Inputs	Outputs	Notes
Clear understanding of objectives [1]	Leader pursues objective-achieving course(s) of action [1]	
Ability to be decisive [1]	Having carefully considered the appropriate course of	

	action, the leader acts decisively even when to do so involves some considerable effort and/or cost [1]
Objective-frustrating events [2]	Leader is resilient in pursuit of objectives [2]
Changing environment and/or priorities [3]	Leader is prepared to abandon a course of action once it becomes clear that it should be (is not influenced by amount of effort and resources already invested) [3]

Informative Notes

Outcome 1 – the leader consistently displays the ability to think and act decisively in pursuit of objective(s).

Outcome 2 – when progress is frustrated the leader consistently displays a willingness to try again until success is achieved.

Outcome 3 – the previous outcome notwithstanding, when it becomes clear that a course of action is no longer viable and the pursuit of which is unwise, the leader rationally evaluates whether continued pursuit is advisable.

General

Action-oriented leaders are able to overcome the inertia and disincentives that reside in situations that others might succumb to. Action-orientation is particularly relevant in goal-frustrating situations when others might give up.

Action-oriented implies taking action when necessary, but also implies refraining from action when none is required – the 'leave well-enough alone' principle. In this way, a leader creates confidence in the group by being calm and in control.

Leaders are more likely to develop resilience when their guiding vision (that they have communicated effectively to the group) is sufficiently strong to supersede the alternative situation that has been imposed on them, and which threatens the realization of the goal. It is having the integrity of character to remain true to the original goal in the face of adversity.

Leaders who appear to lack energy and enthusiasm are likely to very quickly lose the confidence of those they would seek to lead. Even worse than appearing to lack enthusiasm is being seen to be comfortable and accepting of this lack-lustre performance.

Virtual and/or Integrated Teams

In virtual environments individual team members must be encouraged to be pro-active in pursuit of objectives and in the face of frustrating events. The leader can facilitate this by recruiting people with these tendencies in the first place, but also by running periodic exercises in which team members are given a problem with an appropriate scope to solve.

In integrated environments, complexity may lead to indecision and paralysis among team members. The same qualities as with virtual teams are desirable, particularly where an integrated team member is required to act with minimal supervision.

Notes on how to apply in your project(s)

Table 8: IND.4 Action-orientation

C.2.7.5. *IND.5 Intelligence*

Process ID	IND.5	Notes
Process Name:	**Intelligence**	
Process Purpose:	The purpose of the intelligence process is to apply appropriate cognitive resources in the achievement of goals.	
Process Outcomes:	As a result of successful implementation of the intelligence process:	
	1. Original thinking in team-members is facilitated.	
	2. Situations are realistically understood.	
	3. Cause(s) of objective-achieving outcomes are generated.	
Base Practices:	**IND.5.BP1: Facilitate original thinking.** The leader encourages a high-level of original	

thinking in the team,
enabling new solutions
to problems to be
developed, unbounded
by orthodoxy. [1]

**IND.5.BP2: Understand
situations realistically.**
The leader displays a
realistic understanding
of situations, which
enables objective-
achieving action to be
taken [2].

**IND.5.BP3: Create
objective-achieving
causes.** The leader takes
responsibility for
outcomes by consciously
generating the
circumstances or causes
that lead to the events
and outcomes that
support objective(s)
achievement (i.e.
generating the right
conditions for objectives
to be achieved) [3].

Work Products / Activities / Conditions

Inputs	Outputs	Notes
Team environment and climate in which original thinking is encouraged and rewarded [1]	Team members actively pursue original ideas that respond directly to the real challenges of the moment (not automatically a repetition of an orthodox solution) [1]	
Rational, clear thinking evaluation of situations [2]	Leader perceives the most appropriate course of action in pursuit of objectives [2]	
The need to achieve certain outcomes/objectives [3]	Leader consciously engineers events that will have objective-achieving effects [3]	
	Leader takes responsibility for project events, recognising that he/she is ultimately	

---

responsible [3]

Leader avoids
playing the blame-
game, even when
there is some
justification [3]

Informative Notes

Outcome 1 – the leader encourages a high-level of original thinking in the team, enabling new solutions to problems to be developed, unbounded by orthodoxy. This can be achieved by explicitly encouraging thinking beyond the conventional, setting the expectation that this will be so. The leader can reward original thinking. In short, it becomes a group-norm.

Outcome 2 – the leader displays a realistic understanding of situations, which enables appropriate action to be taken. Appropriate in this sense means achievement of objectives.

Outcome 3 – the leader takes responsibility for outcomes by consciously generating the circumstances or causes that lead to the events and outcomes that support objectives achievement. In other words, generating the right conditions for objectives to be achieved.

General

Abstract conceptualization is an aspect of intelligence that allows a leader to mentally manipulate abstractions in problem-solving, efficiency-enhancing ways. This is related to the ability to create a unifying vision for the project, which can be seen as a higher level abstract conceptualization skill. The skill being discussed in this process relates more to how to make it happen.

Without necessarily dispensing with the benefits of accumulated experience and lessons learned, creative, unorthodox thinking can lead to solutions that elude conventional thinking. Persistent problems often require new ways of thinking. Original thinkers are not so influenced by the opinions of those that say 'it cannot be done', they are more likely to think 'we haven't thought of a solution yet'. It is to be free from the restraints of tradition - the 'wisdom of the ages' that can sometimes be a straightjacket for the mind. A leader who brings this approach to leadership allows the team to function naturally, in proper response to the conditions in which it finds itself. A tradition-bound leader will base his decisions on precedent 'what did my predecessors do in this situation'. These prefabricated responses lack insight and run a high risk of not being appropriate for the situation at hand.

Good judgment is a fundamental ability that informs almost all of a leader's activities. It is the foundation of appropriate action. Good judgment is conditional upon a rational, objective mind-set in which people, objects and events are viewed realistically for what they are in any particular set of circumstances, rather than relying on stereotypes and prescribed understandings to guide action.

Accepting responsibility requires the courage to accept the truth/reality of a situation, even when it is unpleasant.

Effective leaders accept that the circumstances in which they find themselves are largely the result of their own previous actions. They do not blame others. They are able to see the linkages between cause and effect, how their behavior affects corporate vision and how their leadership can affect the profitability of the organisation. Effective leaders are proactive, rather than reactive, taking the initiative to improve matters.

Virtual and/or Integrated Teams

In virtual and integrated environments ways must be found to encourage innovative thinking among team members who are not able to bounce ideas off each other in the same physical space. To the extent allowable by the available ICT and groupware, brainstorming sessions are an effective way to foster innovative thinking, as well as creating an environment in which free-thinking is encouraged. The leader should reward and be seen to be rewarding examples of innovative thinking that is directed towards the achievement of objectives.

In **integrated environments** the issue may be one of coordinating meetings of the extended team at a convenient time and place, whether in a co-located or virtual sense.

Appearing to lack the ability to think creatively and being resistant to new ideas will have a seriously negative effect on how you are perceived as a leader. A leader who thinks creatively and is not afraid to make mistakes so long as they learn from them is more likely to be respected and followed.

Notes on how to apply in your project(s)

Table 9: IND.5 Intelligence

C.2.7.6. IND.6 Individualised consideration

Process ID	IND.6	Notes
Process Name:	**Individualised consideration**	
Process Purpose:	The purpose of the individualized consideration process is to convey to team-members their value as individuals.	
Process Outcomes:	As a result of successful implementation of the individualised consideration process:	
	1. Individual team-members are valued	
	2. Individual team-members are unified into team	
	3. Empathy towards individual team-members is practiced	
	4. Objective-achieving team behavior is rewarded	

Base Practices:	**IND.6.BP1: Value the individual.** The leader manifests an understanding of team-members within a mind-set of respect, leading to a valuing of the member as an individual [1]
	IND.6.BP2: Individuals unified into team. The leader engenders a sense of unity (or unified-mind) in the team [2].
	IND.6.BP3: Empathy for individuals. The leader empathises with team members to understand their individual experiences and situation [3].
	IND.6.BP4: Reward object-achieving behavior. The leader encourages individual goal-achieving behavior by positive reinforcement. Negative reinforcement is avoided unless necessary. Absence of positive reinforcement

functions in place of
negative [4].

Work Products / Activities / Conditions

Inputs	Outputs	Notes
Team is a heterogeneous group [1]	Team members are known to the leader as valued individuals [1]	
	Team members do not feel themselves to be mere units of production [1]	
Group is not yet a team (no unified mind-set) [2]	Leader takes action to engender a team mind-set with a unified sense of purpose [2]	
Team members are an unknown [3]	Leader uses empathy to understand the individual team members [3]	
No reward structure exists yet [4]	Leader establishes the practice of positive reinforcement for desirable team behavior, and absence of +ve	

reinforcement for
undesirable behavior.
Negative reinforcement
reserved for extremely
undesirable behavior [4]

Informative Notes

Outcome 1 – the leader manifests an understanding of team-members within a mind-set of respect. This leads to a valuing of the member as an individual. On perceiving this mind-set in the leader, the member's commitment is reinforced.

Outcome 2 – the leader engenders a sense of unity in the team. A 'group-mind' that thinks as one mind. Team-members performance is enhanced by this sense of oneness with the team.

Outcome 3 – the leader empathises with team members to understand their individual experiences and situation. This ability to place oneself 'in the shoes of another' reinforces the perception in the team-member that they are understood and valued.

Outcome 4 – the leader encourages goal-achieving behavior in team by rewarding such behavior. By implication negative reinforcement is avoided unless absolutely necessary. The absence of positive reinforcement functions in place of negative, and avoids resentment build-up in team-members.

General

Team members recognize that the leaders to some extent know them as an individual. The antithesis of this is a team member who feels that the leader regards them as mere units of production, expendable.

An aspect of original thinking is the ability to recognize the individual talents of team members, and unite them into a single enterprise, helping them to develop their own skills and become better people in the process.

Empathy is distinct from sympathy. Sympathy involves becoming emotionally attached to people and outcomes, whereas empathy is dispassionate, non-judgmental. An analogy from the medical domain is that of a doctor using empathy to accurately understand a patient's condition/situation. The doctor cannot sympathise with the patient, unless they are to risk becoming overwhelmed by the suffering they encounter in the course of a day.

In behavioral psychology terms, rewarding desirable performance implies positive reinforcement for desirable behavior. A common mistake is to take desirable performance for granted, effectively ignoring it, while taking action to punish when undesirable performance occurs. While necessary to do the latter on occasion, it must be remembered that the leader's attention is a reward in itself and adopting a reward for desirable performance approach shows significant benefits.

Virtual and/or Integrated Teams

In virtual environments the means by which a leader communicates his/her individualised consideration is the critical issue. If the number of members makes it practical, a one-to-one private conversation every now and then in which the leader gets to know the team member as a whole person can be useful.

If the virtual team member is a self-motivated, well-organised knowledge worker who delivers results not excuses, the frequency of these bonding sessions need not be great. In the event that a team member is experiencing a crisis, the leader may offer support. A chronically crisis-stricken team-member who continually makes excuses for not meeting deadlines may not have a future as a virtual worker.

Notes on how to apply in your project(s)

Table 10: IND.6 Individualised consideration

C.2.7.7. IND.7 Management-by-exception

Process ID	IND.7	Notes
Process Name:	**Management-by-exception**	
Process Purpose:	The purpose of the management-by-exception process is to empower team-members to act independently until and unless non-compliance of standards has occurred.	
Process Outcomes:	As a result of successful implementation of the management-by-exception process: 1. Independent team behavior that is objective-achieving is encouraged 2. Non-objective-achieving team behavior is corrected	
Base Practices:	**IND.7.BP1: Encourage independent, objective-achieving behavior.** When the team is doing their job the leader leaves them alone	

(i.e. the leader avoids the impression of being a 'micro-manager') [1].

IND.7.BP2: Correct non-objective-achieving behavior. The leader takes action to correct the behavior of team members when they engage in non-objective-achieving behavior. [2].

Work Products / Activities / Conditions

Inputs	Outputs	Notes
Team members pursuing their tasks without active supervision group [1]	Having created clear objectives and recruited self-motivated competent people, the leader allows them to pursue the project objectives without micro-management group [1]	
Team member is off-track and/or unproductive [2]	Leader re-establishes objective-achieving behavior in team	

member [2]

Informative Notes

Outcome 1 – when the team is doing their job the leader leaves them alone. In effect, the leader does not give the impression of being a 'micro-manager'. If the team is inexperienced, coaching of specific skills towards objective(s) achievement is warranted. The leader should evaluate the potential negative impact of such coaching before performing.

Outcome 2 – the leader takes action to correct the behavior of team members when they engage in non-objective-achieving behavior. When they have gotten 'off the track' or gone 'off on a tangent'. This corrective action must be done with an attitude of respect, and should not resemble negative reinforcement except in extreme or repeated instances.

General

The 'reward desirable performance' process notwithstanding, under some circumstances, it is appropriate to operate on a management by exception basis. This empowered approach is appropriate when a member is expected to act independently, with a degree of autonomy. The member might be a sub-contractor who maintains a professional approach to his/her work and can be relied upon to perform professionally and to a high standard.

Virtual and/or Integrated Teams

In virtual environments management by exception is often the default condition. Virtual team members are chosen and retained for their ability to get the job done without micro-management. The challenge for the leader is to get the balance right; not too much and not too little supervisory presence in the lives of their virtual workers.

Notes on how to apply in your project(s)

Table 11: IND.7 Management-by-exception

C.2.8. Team Process Group (TEM)

C.2.8.1. TEM.1 Team structure

Process ID	TEM.1	Notes
Process Name:	**Team structure**	
Process Purpose:	The purpose of the team structure process is to create a flexible, goal-oriented team structure.	
Process Outcomes:	As a result of successful implementation of the team structure process: 1. Objective-aligned team structure is established. 2. Adaptable team structure is established.	
Base Practices:	**TEM.1.BP1: Establish objective-aligned team structure.** The leader establishes a team structure that is broadly consistent with the project's objectives and requirements [1]	

TEM.1.BP2: Establish an adaptable team structure.

The leader establishes a structure that is able to dynamically adapt to changeable conditions (i.e. cost, schedule, risk, resource projections, business processes, project's defined process, and organizational guidelines) [2]

Work Products / Activities / Conditions

Inputs	Outputs
Team structure not yet determined [1]	Leader develops a structure in keeping with project objectives [1]
Changeable circumstances put pressure on structure [2]	Leader develops team structure with capability to adapt to changing conditions [2]

Informative Notes

Outcome 1 – the leader establishes a team structure that is broadly consistent with the project's objectives and requirements.

Outcome 2 – the leader establishes a structure that is able to dynamically adapt to changeable conditions (i.e. cost, schedule, risk, resource projections, business processes, the project's defined process, and organizational guidelines).

General

Factors influencing appropriate team structure include product requirements, cost, schedule, risk, resource projections, business processes, the project's defined process, and organizational guidelines. These are evaluated to establish the basis for defining teams and their responsibilities, authorities, and interrelationships.

The Work Breakdown Structure (WBS) and derived product-oriented hierarchy may provide an appropriate team structure. More complex structuring occurs when the WBS is not product-oriented, product risks are not uniform, and resources are constrained.

The team structure is a dynamic entity that is adjusted to changes in people, requirements, and the nature of tasks, and to tackle many difficulties. The team structure should be continuously monitored to detect malfunctions, mismanaged interfaces, and mismatches of the work to the staff.

Virtual and/or Integrated Teams

In virtual and integrated environments there must be sufficient flexibility to add or subtract team members from the virtual project team, as required. Such a team structure should be flexible enough to accommodate change, including changes to team numbers. Virtual teams staffed by external contractors offer the greatest degree of flexibility.

Notes on how to apply in your project(s)

Table 12: TEM.1 Team structure

C.2.8.2.   TEM.2 Team requirements

Process ID	TEM.2	Notes
Process Name:	**Team requirements**	
Process Purpose:	The purpose of the team requirements process is to allocate project requirements to teams.	
Process Outcomes:	As a result of successful implementation of the team requirements process: 1. Team structure is verified. 2. Team sponsor(s) are appointed (Integrated)	
Base Practices:	**TEM.2.BP1: Verify team structure**. The leader verifies the team structure by allocating the project requirements before team members are recruited to verify that the team structure is appropriate to objectives. [1]	

TEM.2.BP2: In integrated environments, team sponsors appointed. In integrated team environments the leader delegates to suitable team sponsor(s) the task of recruiting team members for each of the individual teams within the larger integrated team. [2]

Work Products / Activities / Conditions

Inputs	Outputs	Notes
Project requirements not allocated [1]	Leader allocates requirements to verify that the structure is workable [1]	
	Allocation of requirements is appropriate for the achievement of objectives [1]	
Complex team structure [2]	Leader delegates to sponsors the task of recruiting team leads [2]	

Informative Notes

Outcome 1 – the leader verifies the team structure by allocating the project requirements before team members are recruited to verify that the team structure is appropriate to objectives.

Outcome 2 – in integrated team environments the leader delegates to suitable team sponsor(s) the task of recruiting team members for each of the individual teams within the larger integrated team.

General

This allocation of requirements to teams is done before any teams are formed to verify that the team structure is workable and covers all the necessary requirements, responsibilities, authorities, tasks, and interfaces. Once the structure is confirmed, team sponsors are chosen to establish (recruit) the individual teams in the structure.

Virtual and/or Integrated Teams

In integrated team environments it may be necessary to appoint team sponsors who are chosen to establish (recruit) the individual teams in the structure.

Notes on how to apply in your project(s)

Table 13: TEM.2 Team requirements

C.2.8.3. TEM.3 Team recruitment

Process ID	TEM.3	Notes
Process Name:	**Team recruitment**	
Process Purpose:	The purpose of the team recruitment process is to recruit persons with skills appropriate to the achievement of project goals.	
Process Outcomes:	As a result of successful implementation of the team recruitment process: 1. Team members with appropriate skills are recruited. 2. Virtual team members with appropriate skills are recruited (Virtual) 3. Team leaders consistent with requirements are appointed (Integrated)	
Base Practices:	**TEM.3.BP1: Recruit team members.** The leader recruits team members with	

the requisite skills for the project under consideration. Where the project is complex, a more diverse set of team-member skills will be needed. [1]

TEM.3.BP2: In virtual environments recruit team members. The leader of the virtual team recruits team members with specific personality traits known to function optimally in such environments. [2]

TEM.3.BP3: In integrated environments, team leaders are recruited. In integrated environments the leader delegates to team sponsor(s) the task of recruiting/appointing suitable team-leaders whose capabilities are consistent with the project requirements. [3]

Work Products / Activities / Conditions		
Inputs	Outputs	Notes

Team structure and requirements exists, no staff yet [1]	Leader uses the team structure and allocated requirements to determine who should be recruited [1]
	Diverse skill sets needed for complex projects [1]
Virtual team [2]	Recruit team members with personality traits known to function well in virtual environments [2]
Integrated team [3]	Leader delegates to team sponsors the task of recruiting suitably qualified members [3]

Informative Notes

Outcome 1 – the leader recruits team members with the requisite skills for the project under consideration. Where the project is complex, a more diverse set of team-member skills will be needed.

Outcome 2 – in virtual environments, team members with specific personality traits known to function optimally in such environments are recruited (further discussion in virtual teams informative section below)

Outcome 3 – in integrated environments the leader delegates to team sponsor(s) the task of recruiting/appointing suitable team-leaders whose capabilities are consistent with the project requirements.

General

Geographically dispersed, complex and/or co-located teams will normally require a broad base of potential expertise to be drawn upon when assembling a team. This is particularly true when the task to be performed is a complex one.

Virtual and/or Integrated Teams

Where possible in virtual environments select team members who demonstrate strong loyalty to the organisation (how long have they been employed, are there reasons to not change jobs) and a demonstrated commitment to the vision, goals and objectives of the organisation (ask them what their ideal org would look like).

Virtual team members should be reliable, self-disciplined, adaptable, resourceful, well-organised with advanced problem-solving skills, able to take the initiative, effective at communicating electronically, is able to stay on task and deliver results (not excuses). Virtual workers should have confidence in their abilities, since working alone self-doubt can be a problem. They should be good communicators. The best predictor of future success is often past success.

Desirable in virtual team members is a good sense of humour, since this is an indicator of a person who is slow to anger and therefore better able to deal constructively with the frustrations of the virtual workplace.

Virtual team members can be engaged on the basis of outcomes where said members are external contractors. The terms of engagement are that certain specified outcomes/work products shall be delivered by a certain date for an agreed payment. Further engagement may be on-going subject to satisfactory performance.

Notes on how to apply in your project(s)

Table 14: TEM.3 Team recruitment

C.2.8.4. TEM.4 Team environment

Process ID	TEM.4	Notes
Process Name:	**Team environment**	
Process Purpose:	The purpose of the team environment process is to establish the project's work environment.	
Process Outcomes:	As a result of successful implementation of the team environment process:	
	1. Appropriate infrastructure is provided.	
	2. On-demand, synchronous, hi-resolution communications media is provided (Virtual and/or Integrated).	
	3. On-demand, synchronous, hi-resolution communications media is used (Virtual and/or Integrated).	

Base Practices:	**TEM.4.BP1: Provide appropriate infrastructure.** The leader facilitates the provision of a team environment to include all required physical infrastructure and supporting facilities; from office space to computer and photocopiers (etc). [1]
	TEM.4.BP2: In virtual and/or integrated environments, on-demand, synchronous hi-res communications media is provided. Team-members should if possible have ready access to hi-resolution videoconferencing facilities that are sufficiently richly-textured that participants are able to see the nuances of non-verbal communication in the remote participants. The audio must be high-fidelity enough to hear the nuances of verbal communication. [2]

TEM.4.BP3 In virtual and/or integrated environments, on-demand, synchronous hi-res communications media is used. Team-members in virtual integrated environments are in no doubt that these facilities are available and should be used frequently or at least as often as necessary to maintain a level of contact roughly equivalent to co-located teams who interact face-to-face as required. [3]

Work Products / Activities / Conditions

Inputs	Outputs	Notes
A defined scope of work exists but no infrastructure yet [1]	Leader makes (or delegates) the arrangements for the provision of the required range of team infrastructure. [1]	
Virtual and/or integrated team	Leader makes (or delegates) provision of hi-resolution	

[2]	videoconferencing facilities [2]
Virtual and/or integrated team [3]	Leader (or delegates) ensures the use of hi-resolution videoconferencing facilities [3]

Informative Notes

Outcome 1 – team environment is defined broadly to include all required physical infrastructure and supporting facilities; from office space to computer and photocopiers (etc).

Outcome 2 – team-members should if possible have ready access to hi-resolution videoconferencing facilities that are sufficiently rich-textured that participants are able to see the nuances of non-verbal communication in the remote participants. The audio must be high-fidelity enough to hear the nuances of verbal communication.

Outcome 3 – team-members in virtual integrated environments are in no doubt that these facilities are available and should be used frequently or at least as often as necessary to maintain a level of contact roughly equivalent to co-located teams who interact face-to-face when required.

General

Team members must be in a position to communicate with each other in ways that approximate normal face-to-face interactions. This implies that voice-only telephone and email are insufficient for this purpose. Video telephones and/or web-cam based audio-visual channels that deliver frame-rates that replicate natural movement and speech would be desirable.

Virtual and/or Integrated Teams

Team members in virtual and integrated environments must be in a position to communicate with each other in ways that approximate normal face-to-face interactions. This implies that voice-only telephone and email are insufficient for this purpose. Video telephones and/or web-cam based audio-visual channels that deliver frame-rates that replicate natural movement and speech would be desirable.

It is imperative that a sense of presence is established, making use of appropriate ICT. If this cannot be physical presence, then virtual presence must be substituted to create a sense of ambient awareness and perceived proximity among virtual team members. It is strongly recommended that projects be commenced with a face-to-face meeting of the project team using richly-textured, high-resolution ICT if physical presence is not possible. Team members must become comfortable with and come to regularly use the technology as an established habit. This will foster the formation of interpersonal relationships mediated by the technology. As the leader, you should model this desirable behavior, using the technology in the way you want the team to use it. These relationships between you and the team and between the team members then form the foundation for team performance.

How often to communicate will vary, but as a guide three or

four communications a day is about right, however you should obviously avoid irritating people with too-frequent contact. The objective is to build relationships with two-way communication, being supportive without being intrusive. The communication will be a mixture of project-related and social. Team members should get the impression you know them and value them as whole people, not just objective-achieving units of production (which can be demotivating). Experiment with the available media, and do not discount social networking tools (e.g. Facebook etc).

When issuing orders to team members, try to make the tone of the communication supportive rather than directive, thus creating a greater sense of collaboration.

Notes on how to apply in your project(s)

Table 15: TEM.4 Team environment

C.2.8.5. TEM.5 Team formation

Process ID	TEM.5	Notes
Process Name:	**Team formation**	
Process Purpose:	The purpose of the team formation process is to constitute the team structure.	
Process Outcomes:	As a result of successful implementation of the team formation process:	
	1. Team structure consistent with project requirements is established.	
	2. Team charter consistent with requirements is established.	
	3. Resources consistent with project requirements are allocated.	
Base Practices:	**TEM.5.BP1: Establish team structure consistent with requirements.** The leader (or someone delegated)	

organises team members in
ways that are appropriate
for the project requirements.
[1]

**TEM.5.BP2: Establish team
charter consistent with
requirements.** The leader
develops a team charter
appropriate to the project
requirements. [2]

**TEM.5.BP2: Allocate
resources to the team.** The
leader allocates the
resources necessary to meet
the project requirements.
This includes provision of
necessary goods and
services, and also the
budgetary means by which
teams can be brought
together for project/stage
launches and other team
building exercises. [3]

Work Products / Activities / Conditions		
Inputs	Outputs	Notes
Project requirements have been allocated, team structure verified, team members recruited, yet the team is not yet organised [1]	Leader (or delegate) organises team consistent with requirements [1]	
Team is formed, no charter yet [2]	Leader devises or adapts an existing team charter to reflect the vision and values of the team [2]	
Team is formed, resources not yet allocated [3]	Leader (or delegate) makes arrangements for the necessary resources (goods and services excluding physical infrastructure) [3]	

Informative Notes

Outcome 1 – the leader (or someone delegated) organises team members in ways that are appropriate for the project requirements.

Outcome 2 – the leader develops a team charter appropriate to the project requirements. The team charter must embody the vision and there should be nothing in the charter that runs contrary to the spirit of the vision, either literally or by implication. Team members will be quick to notice any hypocrisy in this regard, and the consequent mistrust and cynicism will have a corrosive effect on team effectiveness.

Outcome 3 – the leader allocates the resources necessary to meet the project requirements. This includes the provision of necessary goods and services, and also the budgetary means by which teams can be brought together for project/stage launches and other team building exercises.

General

With more complex teams, the leader might delegate to the sponsors the task of appointing team leaders and team members, and establishing the team charter for each integrated team based on the allocation of requirements. It also involves providing the resources required to accomplish the tasks assigned to the team.

Virtual and/or Integrated Teams

In virtual and integrated environments team members must be well-organised for the task at hand, understand clearly what is expected of them, and have the means to carry out their assigned tasks.

Notes on how to apply in your project(s)

Table 16: TEM.5 Team formation

C.2.8.6. *TEM.6 Team roles*

Process ID	TEM.6	Notes
Process Name:	**Team roles**	
Process Purpose:	The purpose of the team roles process is to define member roles.	
Process Outcomes:	As a result of successful implementation of the team roles process:	
	1. Team member roles are understood.	
	2. Contingency plans for team member absences are developed.	
	3. Singular roles per member in synchronous virtual environments are defined (Virtual teams only)	
	4. Singular and/or multiple roles per member in asynchronous virtual environments are defined (Virtual & integrated teams).	

Base Practices:	**TEM.6.BP1: Make team roles understood.** The leader ensures everyone clearly understands their roles, particularly those performing multiple roles. Roles are consistent with team structure. [1]

TEM.6.BP2: Develop contingency plan. The leader develops contingency plans for when team members are unavailable for further work [2].

TEM.6.BP3: In virtual environments, synchronous virtual environments, singular roles are allocated to team members (where possible). The leader defines clear, stable and singular team membership roles where tasks are performed synchronously in virtual environments [3]

TEM.6.BP4: In virtual and integrated environments,

asynchronous virtual environments, singular and/or multiple roles may be allocated. The leader has the discretion to define singular and/or multiple roles per member when project operates in asynchronous environments (singular is desirable, but multiple may be unavoidable) [4].

Work Products / Activities / Conditions

Inputs	Outputs	Notes
Team is formed and resourced, individual roles not yet understood by members [1]	Leader briefs each team member as to their specific role(s) [1]	
No contingency plan [2]	Leader devises contingency plans in the event of resources being unexpectedly unavailable [2].	
Virtual team	Leader defines,	

members roles [3]	where possible, clear, stable and singular team membership roles where tasks are performed synchronously in virtual environments [3]
Complex virtual teams [4]	Leader defines, where possible, singular and/or multiple roles in asynchronous environments (singular is desirable, but multiple may be unavoidable) [4].

Informative Notes

Outcome 1 – the leader ensures everyone clearly understands their roles, particularly those performing multiple roles. Roles are consistent with team structure. Sufficient flexibility in role assignments is built in to accommodate the often dynamic nature of team structures.

Outcome 2 – the leader develops contingency plans for when team members are unavailable for further work.

Outcome 3 – where possible, the leader defines clear, stable and singular team membership roles where tasks are performed synchronously in virtual environments.

Outcome 4 – where possible, the leader has the discretion to define singular and/or multiple roles per member when project operates in asynchronous environments.

General

Clearly defined team roles avoid role confusion and wasted effort. The effort expended by the leader on making sure everyone understands their role(s) should rise where members are performing multiple roles and the potential for confusion is high.

Contingency planning for the absence of key resources is recommended, with evidence to suggest such planning affords a high ROI for the leader.

Virtual Team Environments

While virtual team members may on occasion perform multiple roles, it becomes increasingly important that roles are clearly defined when the task complexity increases, and the work is done synchronously. Rigid role definition becomes less important when the tasks are simpler, particularly when the tasks can be performed asynchronously.

When team members hold multiple roles within and across different teams, the leaders performance management job becomes more difficult in the sense that role ambiguity and role conflict are likely to occur. The leader must make clear for each member exactly what their role is, in other words what the leader's expectations are in terms of commitment of time and effort.

Notes on how to apply in your project(s)

Table 17: TEM.6 Team roles

C.2.8.7. TEM.7 Team rules

Process ID	TEM.7	Notes
Process Name:	**Team rules**	
Process Purpose:	The purpose of the team rules process is to establish rules for optimal teams conduct in support of objectives.	
Process Outcomes:	As a result of successful implementation of the team rules process: 1. Criteria for optimal team performance in support of objectives are established. 2. Empowered operating conduct for optimal team performance in support of objectives is established.	
Base Practices:	**TEM.7.BP1: Establish performance criteria.** The leader sets the standard of expected performance so team leaders and members are clear about the standard	

to which they must work [1].

TEM.7.BP2: Establish empowered operating conduct. The leader facilitates optimal team performance in pursuit of the project objectives establishing empowered team member operating conduct. [2].

Work Products / Activities / Conditions

Inputs	Outputs	Notes
Team is formed, roles known, criteria for optimal team performance not yet known [1]	Leader briefs team members as to the expected performance standards [1]	
Optimal performance criteria known, conditions conducive to achieving optimal performance not	Leader creates an environment in which team members are empowered to perform at the expected optimal level [2]	

yet established
[2]

Team members have
the individual
authority to make
decisions that facilitate
optimal performance
for themselves [2]

Informative Notes

Outcome 1 – the leader sets the standard of expected performance so team leaders and members are clear about the standard to which they must work.

Outcome 2 – optimal team performance in pursuit of the project objectives is facilitated by establishing empowered team member operating conduct. The degree of empowerment will depend on the specific nature of a project. Some will need more active supervision, some less.

General

Clearly understood team rules that derive from the team charter give team members a degree of confidence that their activities at any given time are within the prescribed guidelines. This is not to say the rules must never broke. If there is sufficient justifiable cause, team rules can and should be amended to take account of a practical reality that might be different from that which existed when the rules were devised.

Virtual and/or Integrated Teams

In virtual and integrated teams, operating rules and guidelines define and control how teams interact to accomplish objectives. These rules and guidelines also promote the effective leveraging of the teams' efforts, high performance, and productivity. Integrated team members must understand the standards for work and participate according to those standards.

Notes on how to apply in your project(s)

Table 18: TEM.7 Team rules

C.2.8.8. *TEM.8 Team authority*

Process ID	TEM.8	Notes
Process Name:	**Team authority**	
Process Purpose:	The purpose of the team authority process is to create efficiently functioning teams by establishing mechanisms that allows team leaders and members to recognise clear channels of responsibility.	
Process Outcomes:	As a result of successful implementation of the team authority process: 1. Clear channels of responsibility are established. 2. Responsibilities are understood. 3. Team authority and decision-making mechanisms are understood.	

Base Practices:	**TEM.8.BP1: Establish clear channels of responsibility.** The leader creates clear and unambiguous channels of authority and responsibility within the team hierarchy. This is particularly important with integrated teams where a complex team structure exists [1]
	TEM.8.BP2: Ensure responsibilities are understood. The leader communicates these channels of authority and responsibility to all team-leaders and members. Again, this is particularly important with integrated teams where a complex team structure exists [2].
	TEM.8.BP3: Ensure team authority and decision-making mechanisms are understood. The leader communicates the mechanics of team authority and decision-making works,

and how they apply to all
team-leaders and members.
Everyone should
understand how and why
decisions are made. [3].

Work Products / Activities / Conditions

Inputs	Outputs	Notes
Team rules are established, clear channels of responsibility not yet established [1]	Leader communicates unambiguous channels of responsibility to team members [1]	
Channels of responsibility established, not yet clearly understood [2].	Leader ensures team responsibilities are understood by all [2].	
Responsibilities understood by team, decision-making mechanisms not yet clearly understood [3]	Leader ensures all team members understand how and why decisions are made [3]	

Informative Notes

Outcome 1 – the leader creates clear and unambiguous channels of authority and responsibility within the team hierarchy. This is particularly important with integrated teams where a complex team structure exists.

Outcome 2 – the leader communicates these channels of authority and responsibility to all team-leaders and members. Again, this is particularly important with integrated teams where a complex team structure exists.

Outcome 3 – the leader communicates how team authority and decision-making works, the mechanics of it, and how they apply to all team-leaders and members. Everyone should understand how and why decisions are made. This understanding empowers team members to make decisions about the conduct of their own role with greater confidence and a sense of identification with the team as a whole.

General

Teaming introduces challenges to leadership because of the cultural changes required when people and integrated teams are empowered and decisions are driven to the lowest level appropriate. Effective and efficient communication mechanisms are critical to timely and sound decision making in the integrated work environment. Once an integrated team project structure is established and training is provided, mechanisms to handle empowerment, decision making, and issue resolution also need to be provided.

Virtual and/or Integrated Teams

In virtual environments with flat management structures (no middle management) the matter of team authority will be relatively straightforward. A virtual team member reports to the manager, and understands that the other team members are peers. With virtual teams that do have middle management, the nature and scope of these middle managers or team leaders must be well-understood by all.

Notes on how to apply in your project(s)

Table 19: TEM.8 Team authority

C.2.8.9. TEM.9 Team performance management

Process ID	TEM.9	Notes
Process Name:	Team performance management	
Process Purpose:	The purpose of the team performance management process is to manage team performance through the development of empowered performance-management functions that allow team members to manage themselves.	
Process Outcomes:	As a result of successful implementation of the vision process: 1. Self-managing performance functions are developed. 2. High-capability self-managing performance functions for complex asynchronous tasks are developed. 3. Anticipatory self-	

management functions for proactive adaptation to change are developed.

4. Higher-capability self-managing performance functions across complex team boundaries are developed. (Virtual & integrated teams)

Base Practices:	**TEM.9.BP1: Develop self-managing performance functions.** The leader develops explicit performance management functions early in the project lifecycle that allow team members to self-manage their performance. [1]
	TEM.9.BP2: Develop high-capability self-managing performance functions where complex asynchronous tasks are performed. The leader develops higher-order performance self-management functions

where it is necessary to perform complex tasks asynchronously. This condition represents a situation of heightened need for effective self-management of performance by team members [2]

TEM.9.BP3: Develop anticipatory self-management functions. The leader develops performance management functions that anticipate change, and proactively adapts the self-managing team-member to changing environmental conditions [3].

TEM.9.BP4: In virtual environments, develop higher-capability self-managing performance functions where complex team boundaries exist. The leader develops higher-order performance self-management functions where it is necessary to perform tasks in virtual environments with complex team boundaries. This condition represents a situation of heightened need for effective self-management [4].

Work Products / Activities / Conditions

Inputs	Outputs	Notes
Team rules and authority established, self-managing performance management functions not yet established [1]	Self-managing performance functions are adopted by team members [1]	
Complex tasks being performed asynchronously [2]	Higher capability self-managing performance functions are adopted by team members [2]	
Self-managing performance functions in place,	Self-management functions are adaptable to	

but not proactively adaptable to foreseeable change [3]	foreseeable changes [3]
In virtual environments with complex boundaries, self-managing performance functions in place, but not of a higher level capability [4]	Higher-order self-management functions in complex virtual environments where boundary confusion is a risk [4]

Informative Notes

Outcome 1 – the leader develops explicit performance management functions early in the project lifecycle that allow team members to self-manage their performance. Self-management is defined broadly, and might include methods such as the daily team scrum to create a mind-set that help members synchronise their individual efforts for the rest of the day.

Outcome 2 – the leader develops higher-order performance self-management functions where it is necessary to perform complex tasks asynchronously. This condition represents a situation of heightened need for effective self-management of performance by team members.

Outcome 3 -- the leader develops performance management

functions that anticipate change, and proactively adapts the self-managing team-member to changing conditions.

Outcome 4 – the leader develops higher-order performance self-management functions where it is necessary to perform tasks in virtual environments with complex team boundaries. This condition represents a situation of heightened need for effective self-management of performance by complex virtual team members.

General

Where temporal distribution degrades the quality of the information that a leader normally uses to carry out performance management, compensatory measures should be established that (a) allow team members to effectively manage their own performance, and (b) have an anticipatory element that helps team members to avoid potential problems and adapt to changing environmental conditions.

Virtual and/or Integrated Teams

In virtual environments where temporal distribution degrades the quality of the information that a leader normally uses to carry out performance management, compensatory measures should be established that allow team members to effectively manage their own performance, particularly where virtual teams cross multiple boundaries (in terms of culture, organization and specific job functions) it is important for leaders to carefully assess the nature of these boundaries and to determine how best to tailor performance management for individual team members given the nature of the differences.

Notes on how to apply in your project(s)

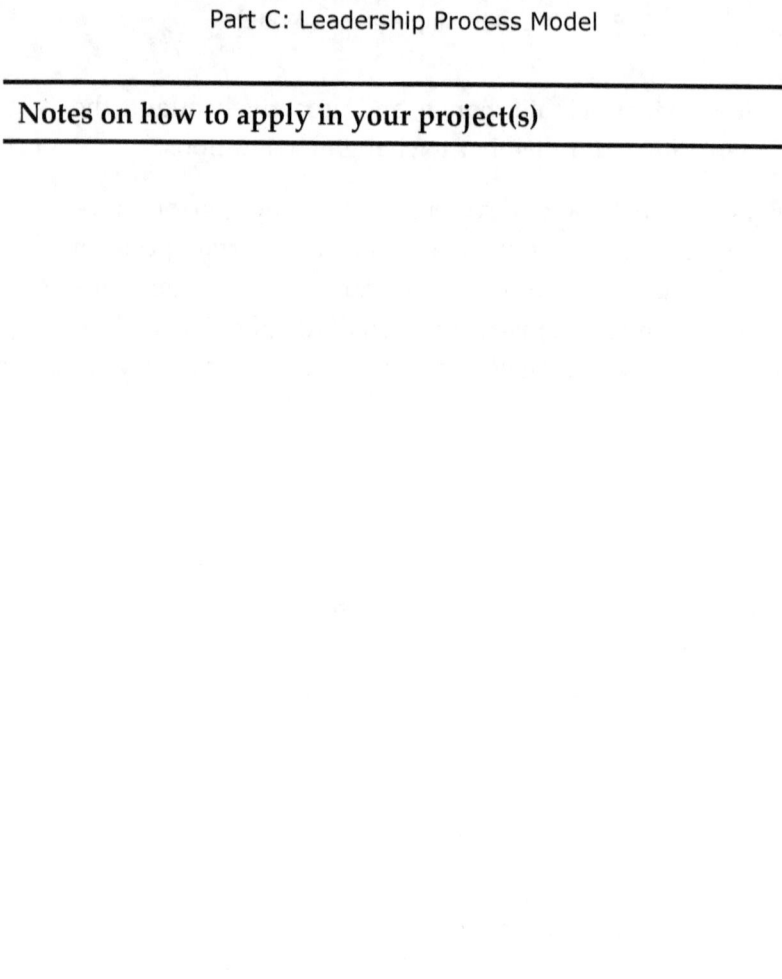

Table 20: TEM.9 Team performance management

C.2.8.10. TEM.10 Team development

Process ID	TEM.10	Notes
Process Name:	**Team development**	
Process Purpose:	The purpose of the team development process is to establish team development functions to promote productivity and coherence.	
Process Outcomes:	As a result of successful implementation of the team development process: 1. Development practices for team coherence are established. 2. Stable team membership is maintained.	
Base Practices:	**TEM.10.BP1: Establish development practices to promote coherence.** The leader of both short-term and long-term projects establishes effective team development functions early in the project lifecycle. In the	

case of short-term projects,
this facilitates the timely
completion of the project.
With long-term projects, this
is the establishment of long-
term working relationships
and complex workflow
arrangements. [1]

**TEM.10.BP2: Maintain
stable team membership.**
The leader maintains stable
team membership. A greater
degree of team membership
stability is desirable where
complex tasks are performed
in virtual environments [2].

Work Products / Activities / Conditions

Inputs	Outputs	Notes
Teams are highly functional, but coherence-enhancing team development functions not yet established [1]	Leader establishes team development functions designed to promote team coherence [1]	

| Teams highly functional, but stability of membership not established [2] | Leader maintains stable team membership [2] |

Informative Notes

Outcome 1 – the leader of both short-term and long-term projects establishes effective team development functions early in the project lifecycle. In the case of short-term projects, this facilitates the timely completion of the project. With long-term projects, this is the establishment of long-term working relationships and complex workflow arrangements.

Outcome 2 – the leader maintains stable team membership. A greater degree of team membership stability is desirable where complex tasks are performed in virtual environments.

General

It is important for both short and long-term projects that the critical team development functions are established as early as possible. For short-term, discrete lifecycle projects, there is usually only time to focus on the most critical of functions, for example effective working relationships.

For long-term, continuous lifecycle projects, these functions are even more important in the sense that stable long-term working relationships are usually required, performing work of a complex nature that requires complex workflow arrangements. Such projects usually require reciprocal workflow arrangements in which integrated teams work collaboratively

Team development activities that promote coherence are likely to be more important when the virtual team operates in real-time. Virtual team leaders are adept at identifying appropriate technology to facilitate the necessary degree of team coherence to achieve success.

Complex tasks require more stable team membership to enable the virtual team to achieve the projects objective(s). Less complex tasks may be more tolerant to dynamic team membership.

Virtual and/or Integrated Teams

In virtual environments with short duration projects, team development need only be minimal. Team members are chosen specifically for the skills they already possess and can use in the realisation of the vision. In longer-term virtual projects, involving people who are employed by the same parent organisation, team development in keeping with the parent's existing staff development policies are a minimum, with additional development (such as training in the use of technology) being applied as might be indicated.

Notes on how to apply in your project(s)

Table 21: TEM.10 Team development

C.2.9. Organisational Process Group (ORG)

C.2.9.1. ORG.1 Team boundaries

Process ID	ORG.1	Notes
Process Name:	**Team boundaries**	
Process Purpose:	The purpose of the team boundaries process is to manage team boundaries.	
Process Outcomes:	As a result of successful implementation of the team boundaries process: 1. Team boundaries are managed. 2. Blended team culture is facilitated.	
Base Practices:	**ORG.1.BP1: Manage team boundaries**. The leader ensures that boundaries concerning functional, organisational, and cultural matters are maintained in a stable and well-defined	

manner in pursuit of project objectives. The more complex the project, the more important that role boundary definition is stable and well-understood by all, thus minimising the potential for confusion [1]

ORG.1.BP2: Facilitate blended team culture. The leader manages team boundaries where teams cross cultures by facilitating an adaptive blended culture based on mutual respect, trust and reciprocity. Said blended culture is an amalgamation of the source cultures, elements of which are adapted to make a culture that is functionally able to accomplish the project objectives, and realise the vision [2].

Work Products / Activities / Conditions

Inputs	Outputs	Notes
Team is fully	Leader manages	

functional internally, but boundaries with other organisational units not yet managed in ways that promote stability and high-performance [1]	organisational boundaries by liaising with management of other organisational units [1]
Team boundaries cross cultures [2]	Leader engenders blended team culture that adaptively combines cultural elements from the constituent members [2]

Informative Notes

Outcome 1 – the leader ensures that boundaries concerning functional, organisational, and cultural matters are maintained in a stable and well-defined manner in pursuit of project objectives. The more complex the project, the more important that role boundary definition is stable and well-understood by all, thus minimising potential for confusion.

Outcome 2 – the leader manages team boundaries where teams cross cultures by facilitating an adaptive blended culture based on mutual respect, trust and reciprocity. Said blended culture is an amalgamation of the source cultures, elements of which are adapted to make a culture that is functionally able to accomplish the project objectives, and realise the vision.

General

Managing team boundaries in a way that allows complex tasks to be performed by teams requires that the boundaries be in a condition that allows defined operating procedures and stable relationships to be maintained. This implies that the boundaries are less changeable over the course of the project lifecycle. Simpler tasks may be more tolerant to change where people move into and out of the team and where explicit operating procedures are less critical.

Teams that span diverse functional, organizational and/or cultural boundaries will have poor cohesion unless the leader works to establish a common culture that is a blend of each member's individual culture. From this basis of common culture, team cohesion can be established and cultivated in a way that develops mutual respect, trust and reciprocity (mutual obligation).

Virtual and/or Integrated Teams

In virtual and team environments the issue of team boundaries is critical. Poorly defined boundaries produce role confusion, wasted effort, poor morale and low productivity. Blended culture between culturally divers virtual team members needs careful attention, since the instinctive xenophobia of people generally tends to group culturally different people into the "them" category of potential enemy. Cultural and/or racial intolerance within virtual teams will have a devastating effect if not carefully managed.

Notes on how to apply in your project(s)

Table 22: ORG.1 Team boundaries

C.2.9.2. ORG.2 Team collaboration

Process ID	ORG.2	Notes
Process Name:	**Team collaboration**	
Process Purpose:	The purpose of the team collaboration process is to ensure effective collaboration among interfacing team elements.	
Process Outcomes:	As a result of successful implementation of the team collaboration process: 1. Environment for collaboration is established. 2. Environment for integrated and/or virtual team collaboration is established (Virtual and Integrated Teams)	
Base Practices:	**ORG.2.BP1: Establish environment for collaboration.** The leader sets up an environment conducive to efficient collaboration. This will	

include morale-building activities, getting-to-know-you exercises, sessions in which the project vision is presented and reinforced in order to build enthusiasm for the realisation of the vision. This may also include the provision of groupware designed to improve the collaborative capabilities of project teams [1]

ORG.2.BP1: In virtual and/or integrated environments, establish environment for collaboration. The leader sets up the mechanisms by which the disparate elements of virtual and/or integrated teams can be made to function smoothly together (for example an Interface Control Group or Committee supported by hi-res ICT) [2].

Work Products / Activities / Conditions		
Inputs	**Outputs**	**Notes**
Team is fully functional internally, and boundaries with other organisational units are being managed, but optimum conditions for collaboration do not yet exist [1]	Leader establishes optimal organisational environment for collaboration with other organisational units [1]	
In virtual and/or integrated environments [2]	Leader establishes mechanisms to unify disparate team elements [2]	

Informative Notes

Outcome 1 – the leader sets up an environment conducive to efficient collaboration. This will include morale-building activities, getting-to-know-you exercises, sessions in which the project vision is presented and reinforced in order to build enthusiasm for the realisation of the vision. This may also include the provision of groupware designed to improve the collaborative capabilities of project teams.

Outcome 2 – the leader sets up the mechanisms by which the disparate elements of virtual and/or integrated team can be made to function smoothly together (for example an Interface Control Group or Committee supported by hi-res ICT).

General

The success of any project depends on how effectively teams collaborate with one another to achieve project objectives.

Virtual and/or Integrated Teams

The success of virtual and/or integrated team-based projects is a function of how effectively and successfully the teams collaborate with one another to achieve project objectives. This collaboration may be accomplished using interface control working groups in the case of integrated teams.

Notes on how to apply in your project(s)

Table 23: ORG.2 Team collaboration

C.2.9.3. ORG.3 Team & home organisation balance

Process ID	ORG.3	Notes
Process Name:	**Team and home organisation balance**	
Process Purpose:	The purpose of the team and home organization process is to balance team and home organization responsibilities.	
Process Outcomes:	As a result of successful implementation of the team and home organization process:	
	1. Guidelines for balancing team and home organization responsibilities are established.	
	2. Guidelines for balancing team and home organization responsibilities are maintained.	

Base Practices:	**ORG.3.BP1: Establish guidelines for team and home organisation balance**. The leader provides guidelines that make clear how team-leaders and members can successfully balance their responsibilities to both team and home organisation [1].
	ORG.3.BP1: Maintain guidelines for team and home organisation balance. The leader maintains said guidelines as the organisational environment evolves. [2].

Work Products / Activities / Conditions

Inputs	Outputs	Notes
Where team members have dual responsibilities to team and home organisation and guidelines for	Leader establishes guidelines for team members to successfully maintain a balance between team and home organisation	

maintaining balance does not yet exist [1]	responsibilities [1]
Where project is longer term, guidelines are subject to change [2]	Leader maintains guidelines for team members to successfully maintain a balance between team and home organisation responsibilities [2]

Informative Notes

Outcome 1 – the leader provides guidelines that make clear how team-leaders and members can successfully balance their responsibilities to both team and home organisation.

Outcome 2 – guidelines will need to be maintained over time as the organisational environment evolves. For example, the issue of work-life balance is attracting a greater degree of importance as time goes by and society expects that people be allowed to 'have a life' outside of their work instead of being defined by their job title. So it is that within an organisation, the guidelines by which people balance their project activities with their larger organisational duties will probably change over time.

General

A 'home organization' is the part of the organization to which team members are assigned when they are not on a specific project team. A home organization may be called a 'functional organization,' 'home base,' 'home office,' or 'direct organization.' Home organizations are often responsible for the career growth of their members (e.g., performance appraisals and training to maintain functional and discipline expertise).

In a team environment, reporting procedures and rating systems assume that members' responsibilities are focused on the project team, not on the home organization. However, the responsibility of team members to their home organizations is also important, specifically for process implementation and improvement. Workloads and responsibilities should be balanced between projects and functions, and between career growth and advancement. Organizational mechanisms should exist that support the home organization while aligning the workforce to meet business objectives in a teaming environment.

Sometimes teams persist beyond their productive life in organizations that do not have a home organization for the team members to return to after the integrated the team is dissolved. Therefore, there should be guidelines for disbanding the integrated teams and maintaining home organizations.

Virtual and/or Integrated Teams

In virtual environments with short duration projects this issue is unlikely to be problematic. In longer-term virtual projects, involving people who are employed by the same parent organisation, the guidelines for managing balance must be in keeping with the parent's existing policies.

Additional guidelines may be necessary if the parent's policies have not caught up with the issue of virtual work.

Frequent communication between the leader and team members using appropriate ICT helps to keep the project firmly in team member's minds when other duties compete for their time and attention

Notes on how to apply in your project(s)

Table 24: ORG.3 Team & home organisation balance

D. References

[1] Eisenhower, D. D. (1988). *The Eisenhower Diaries*. Edited by Robert H. Ferrell. New York: Norton.

[2} Yukl, G., (1994). *Leadership in Organisations*. Englewood Cliffs, N.J. Prentice-Hall.

[3] Bennis, W. and Nanus, B., (1985). *Leaders: the strategies for taking charge*. New York, Haper and Row.

[4] Drucker, P. (1996). *Managing in a Time of Great Change*, Butterworth Heinemann, London.

[5] Bennis, W. (1994). On Becoming a Leader, *What Leaders Read 1*, Perseus Publishing, p 2.

[6] Takala, T., (1998). *Plato on Leadership*. Journal of Business Ethics 17: pp. 785-798

[7] Repenning, N.P., Sterman, J.D., (1997). *Getting Quality the Old-Fashioned Way: Self-Confirming Attributions in the Dynamics of Process Improvement*. Sloan School of Management, MIT., Cambridge, MA. (Available at: http://web.mit.edu/jsterman/www/SDG/Attrib.pdf)

[8] Humphrey, W.S., (2002). *Winning with Software*. Addison Wesley Longman, Reading Massachusetts.

[9] Deming, W.E., (2000). *Out of the Crisis*, MIT Press, Cambridge MA.

[10] Sheard, S.A. (2001). *Evolution of the Framework's Quagmire*, Computer, vol. 34, no. 7, July 2001, pp. 96-98.

[11] Box, G.E.P., (1979). *Robustness in the strategy of scientific model building, in Robustness in Statistics,* R.L. Launer and G.N. Wilkinson, Editors. Academic Press: New York.

[12] ISO/IEC TR 24774 (2007). Software and systems engineering -- Life cycle management -- Guidelines for process description. This Standard was published in 2007.

[13] ISO/IEC 15504 (2003). *Information Technology: Process Assessment.* Joint Technical Committee IT-015, Software and Systems Engineering. This Standard was published on 2 June 2005.

[14] Humphrey, W.S., (2000). *Introduction to the Team Software Process.* Addison Wesley Reading Massachusetts, p19.

[15] Herbsleb, J. Moitra, D., (2001). *Global Software Development,* IEEE Software, Vol 18, Issue 2, (16-20).

[16] Zaleznik, A., (2004*). Managers and Leaders: Are they different?*, Harvard Business Review, The Best of HBR edition, January. Article first published in 1977.

[17] Gemmill, G., Oakley, J., (1992). Leadership: An alienating social myth?, Human Relations, Vol. 45, Issue 2 pp. 113-129.

[18] Bennis W., Beiderman P. (1997). Organizing Genius: The Secrets of Creative Collaboration. Addison-Wesley.

[19] Bennis, W. (1999a). *The Leadership Advantage, Leader to Leader,* 12, p 12

[20] Bennis, W. (1999b), *Five Competencies of New Leaders, Executive Excellence,* 16 (7), pp.4-5.

[21] Offerman, L.R., Hanges, P.J. & Day, D.V. (2001). *Leaders, followers, and values; progress and prospects for theory and research, The Leadership Quarterly,* 12, pp. 129-131.

[22] Davis, T., Landa, M.J. (1999). *The Trust Deficit, Canadian Manager,* 21(1), pp. 10-27.

[23] Branham, L. (2005). The *7 Hidden Reasons Employees Leave,* American Management Association, 1st Edition, pp 19-20.

[24] Humphrey, W.S., (1997). *Managing Technical People: innovation, teamwork, and the software process.* Addison Wesley Longman, Reading Massachusetts.

[25] Champy, J. (2003), *The Hidden Qualities of Great Leaders, Fast Company Magazine,* 76, p 2.

[26] Macaluso, J. (2003). *Harnessing the Power of Emotional Intelligent Leadership,* The CEO Refresher, p 2.

[27] Zhang, S., Fjermestad, J., Tremaine, M., (2005). *Leadership Styles in Virtual Team Context: Limitations, Solutions and Propositions,* Proceedings of the 38th Hawaii International Conference on System Sciences.

[28] Bass, B., (1985). *Leadership and Performance beyond Expectations,* New York: The Free Press.

[29] Bass, B., Avolio, B. Goodheim, L., (1987). *Biography and the Assessment of Transformational Leadership at the World Class Level,* Journal of Management, vol. 13, pp. 7-19.

[30] Lowe, K., Kroeck K., Sivasubramaniam, N, (1996). Effectiveness Correlates of Transformational and Transactional Leadership: a Meta-analytic Review of the MLQ Literature, Leadership Quarterly, vol. 7, pp. 385-425.

[31] Bass, B, (1990). *Bass and Stodgill's Handbook of Leadership,* New York: Free Press.

[32] Bass, B., Avolio, B., (1993). *Transformational Leadership: A response to Critiques,* in M. M. Chemers & R. Ayman (Eds.), Leadership theory and research: Perspectives and directions, pp. 49-80, San Diego, CA: Academic Press.

[33] Kahai, S., Sosik, J. and Avolio, B. (1997). Effects of Leadership Style and Problem Structure on Work Group Process and Outcomes in an Electronic Meeting System Environment, Personnel Psychology, vol. 50, pp. 1-146.

[34] George, J., Easton, G. Jr., Nunamaker, J., and Northcraft, G., (1990). *A Study of Collaborative Work with and without Computer-based Support,* Information Systems Research, vol. 1, pp. 394-415.

[35] Ho, T., Raman, K., (1997). *The Effect of GSS and Elected Leadership on Small Group Meetings,* Journal of Management Information Systems, vol. 23, pp. 409-472.

[36] Lim, L., Raman, K., Wei, K., (1994). *Interacting Effects of GSS and Leadership,* Decision Support System, vol. 12, pp. 199-1.

[37] Avolio, B., Kahai, S., George, E., (2000). *E-leadership: Implications for Theory, Research, and Practice,* Leadership Quarterly, vol. 11, pp.615-668.

[38] McColl-Kennedy, J., Anderson, R., (2002). Subordinate manager Gender Combination and Perceived Leadership Style Influence on Emotions, Self-esteem and Organizational Commitment, Journal of Business Research, vol. 13, pp 545-559.

[39] O'Leary, M., Orlikowski, W. J., & Yates, J. (2002). *Distributed work over the centuries: Trust and control in the Hudson's Bay Company, 1670–1826.* In P. Hinds & S. Kiesler (Eds.), Distributed Work: 27–54. Cambridge, MA: MIT Press.

[40] Ahuja, M. K., Carley, K., & Galletta, D. F. (1997). *Individual performance in distributed design groups: An empirical study.* Paper presented at the SIGCPR Conference, San Francisco. p 165.

[41] Cascio, W., Shurygailo, S., (2003). *E-Leadership and Virtual Teams, Organizational Dynamics,* vol. 31, pp. 362-376.

[42] DuBrin, A., Dalglish, C., Miller, P (2006). *Leadership,* John Wiley, Australia, 2nd Edition, Brisbane.

[43] Skryme, D., (1998). *Measuring the Value of Knowledge,* Business Intelligence Limited, Wimbledon, United Kingdom.

[44] Bell, B.S., Kozlowski, S.W. (2002). *A Typology of Virtual Teams: Implications for Effective Leadership.* Group and Organisational Management, Vol. 27, No.1 pp. 14-19.

[45] Holmstrom, H., Fitzgerald, B., Agerfalk, P., Conchuir, E., (2006). *Agile Practices Reduce Distance in Global Software Development.* Information Systems Management; Summer 200623;3, p 9.

[46] Ancona, D., Malone, T., Orlikowski, W., Senge, P. (2007). *In Praise of the Incomplete Leader*, Harvard Business Review; Feb2007, Vol. 85 Issue 2, pp. 92-100.